2/6

CHRISTIAN DOCTRINE

CHRISTIAN DOCTRINE

Eight Lectures delivered
in the University of Cambridge
to undergraduates of
all Faculties

by

J. S. WHALE
D.D.

Head Master of Mill Hill School

CAMBRIDGE
AT THE UNIVERSITY PRESS
1952

PUBLISHED BY
THE SYNDICS OF THE CAMBRIDGE UNIVERSITY PRESS

London Office: Bentley House, N.W. 1
American Branch: New York

Agents for Canada, India, and Pakistan: Macmillan

First edition	*August*	1941
Second impression	*November*	1941
Third impression	*January*	1942
Religious Book Club edition	*May*	1942
Fourth impression	*July*	1942
Fifth impression	*November*	1942
Sixth impression		1950
Seventh impression		1952

Printed in Great Britain at the University Press, Cambridge
(Brooke Crutchley, University Printer)

Dedicated
to

CHARLES HAROLD DODD

and to the memory of

JAMES VERNON BARTLET

the teachers to whom I owe most for my
understanding of Christian Truth

CONTENTS

PREFACE

This book reproduces and slightly expands eight lectures delivered in the University of Cambridge during the Michaelmas Term 1940 at the request of the Board of the Faculty of Theology. The lectures were intended for men and women of all Faculties, about six hundred of whom attended them throughout.

I have hesitated to publish these lectures in their original form because the spoken word runs an obvious risk by appearing in print. The kind importunity of many of my hearers has persuaded me, however, and I have gratefully accepted an offer of publication from the Syndics of the University Press.

If the title of the volume looks a little pretentious I must admit that these lectures offer neither a systematic nor a comprehensive survey of Christian doctrine; indeed, I am well aware of their many omissions, and of weaknesses which considerable expansion might have removed. On the other hand an outline of a great subject may have interest and value for many who have neither inclination nor leisure for the study of a fuller and more technical book.

I have to thank the Editor of the *Expository Times* for permission to incorporate material from articles recently contributed to that journal, and the Student Christian Movement Press for allowing me to make use of certain paragraphs from two previous books; details are given in the footnotes.

My other obligations are many and obvious, but I am particularly indebted to Mr B. L. Manning, M.A., Senior Tutor

9

of Jesus College, and to the Rev. H. C. Carter, M.A., Minister of Emmanuel Church, Cambridge, for the pains they have taken in reading my manuscript and pointing out some of its infelicities of style and statement. I wish to thank Mr L. A. Pars, M.A., of Jesus College, for his valuable critical notes on one or two points. It would be almost impertinent to praise the readers and printers of the Cambridge University Press. I can only thank them for a meticulous accuracy which has been an education.

J. S. W.

CHESHUNT COLLEGE
January 1941

I

THE LIVING GOD

THE CHRISTIAN DOCTRINE OF CREATION

A YOUNG curate once called on William Stubbs, Bishop of Oxford, to ask him for advice about preaching. The great man was silent for a moment and then replied 'Preach about God; and preach about twenty minutes'. He meant, presumably, that the Christian preacher has many opportunities, but one theme. So, too, all lectures on Christian doctrine are concerned from first to last with the reality, nature and purpose of the living God.

But is there a God? Apparently not. God is not apparent to our senses. Nor is he indubitably apparent to human reason. The most eager theist knows that the classic arguments for the existence of God, even when restated, are arguments rather than proofs. Again, it is not compellingly apparent that God is the only possible explanation of human history; the problem of evil is a monument to facts which seem to deny it. Nevertheless, belief in the reality of God is the alpha and omega of the Christian religion. Christian doctrines presuppose and illustrate the fundamental doctrine that God is, and that man's chief end is to know him. Look, for example, at six of those doctrines.

The Christian answer to the ageless question, 'What is Man?' is not that man is a thinking animal or a tool-using animal, a cooking animal or a laughing animal.[1] These classic

[1] 'I told him, I had found out a perfect definition of human nature, as distinguished from the animal. An ancient philosopher said, Man

definitions have an obvious validity; but Christian anthropology rests on the conviction that man is an animal made in the image of God, which means that he is not an animal at all. His alleged evolution from mammalian stock, a theory which the biological evidence seems to require, does not affect the truth that he has his origin and essential being in a Word addressed to him by God, his Creator.

The Christian way of thinking about moral evil—all the horrifying and abiding depths of wrong in the human situation —is that moral evil can never have a purely manward reference. Moral evil is sin; more than a private thing like vice, and more than a social or public thing like crime, sin is moral evil seen in its relation to God.

The Christian way out of man's moral distress is not the Greek way of knowledge (ἐπιστήμη); that is, redemption from ignorance. Nor is it the ancient Egyptian way of redemption from mortality, with its elaborate ritual centred in the embalmed mummy and set forth in the *Book of the Dead*. Nor, again, is it the Buddhist way of self-elimination set out in the doctrine of Nirvana. The Christian religion understands redemption in terms of moral realities; sin and guilt, judgment and grace. Its primary and permanent emphasis is ethical. If salvation is to be real, therefore, God and God alone must

was "a two-legged animal without feathers", upon which his rival Sage had a Cock plucked bare, and set him down in the school before all the disciples, as a "Philosophick Man". Dr Franklin said, Man was "a tool-making animal", which is very well; for no animal but man makes a thing, by means of which he can make another thing. But this applies to very few of the species. My definition of *Man* is, "a Cooking animal". The beasts have memory, judgment, and all the faculties and passions of our mind in a certain degree; but no beast is a cook' (Boswell's *Journal of a Tour to the Hebrides with Samuel Johnson* (August 15)).

effect it; if it is to be anything more than a fiction, it must be the work of him who is of purer eyes than to behold iniquity. The agonizing quest of a Paul, a Luther, a Bunyan for reconciliation with God, meant that nothing less and nothing else could meet their case. The Christian doctrine of redemption can mean one thing only, namely that the Holy One is gracious.

The Christian way of understanding Jesus Christ the Saviour is to worship him as divine. Christian doctrine does not speak of him as history speaks of Aristotle or Buddha, of Socrates or Confucius. He is more than teacher, reformer or prophet. That God was in Christ is the very basis and *raison d'être* of Christian doctrine. To the question, 'Is not this the carpenter?' its answer is 'Behold the Lamb of God'.

The Christian way of understanding the society which is the result and the extension in time of what Christ was and what he did, is not that it is just one among many forms of human association, something of man's contriving, an expression of human idealism whose *differentia* is mainly sociological. The Church is a wonderful and sacred mystery because God loved it, Christ purchased it and the Holy Spirit sanctifies it. The minister of the Word and the Sacraments is a steward of the mysteries of God.

The Christian way of understanding history is not the secular way, either of optimism or pessimism. For Christian doctrine, the pattern of history is not expressible in terms of evolutionary progress and human perfectibility here on earth, but in terms of creation and resurrection from the dead. In the beginning God created; in the end he will sum up all things, in heaven and on earth, in Christ. To conceive of a beginning in time is, admittedly, as impossible as to conceive of no beginning.

Again, an end to time is as inconceivable as an endless eternity. The Christian doctrine of creation is a symbolic assertion, not that the world was made by the Great Artificer as a carpenter makes a box, but that man in all his felt finitude comes from God and goes to God; he is not surrounded by a sheer abyss of nothingness. God, the God and Father of our Lord Jesus Christ, is the ground and goal of all that is. All is of God— our creation, preservation and all the blessings of this life; the redemption of the world, the means of grace and the hope of glory. He is the first and the last and the living One.

In short, all Christian doctrines are the same doctrine, the doctrine of God.

At once we meet a notorious difficulty which is illustrated and, as I hope to show, exaggerated by the unhappy divisions of Christendom. How is God known? What is the source of Christian knowledge and the authoritative foundation of Christian doctrine? What is the ultimate seat of authority to which Christian theology makes its appeal?

To these questions Christian history provides answers which are by no means uniform; they fall, in the main, into three great and distinctive types.

The first type emphasizes the authority of the Church, a visible, hierarchical institution, which is the divinely commissioned vehicle and guarantee of the truth and the grace of the Gospel. Such ecclesiasticism becomes nakedly explicit in the unyielding Latin dictum that there is no salvation outside the Church. The Roman Church, indeed, provides the classic form of this deification of the traditional institution, its ruler claiming to be God's Vicar upon earth. When he speaks *ex cathedra*, his pronouncements are infallible. The Vatican

Decrees of 1870 are no more than the logical climax of a long historical development.[1]

The second type emphasizes the sole authority of the Bible, and here historic Protestantism provides the classic example. *The Westminster Confession* (i. 6) is typical of all the credal confessions of the Reformation in saying that 'the whole counsel of God concerning all things necessary for His own glory, man's salvation, faith and life, is either expressly set down in Scripture or by good and necessary consequence may be deduced from Scripture: unto which nothing at any time is to be added, whether by new revelations of the Spirit or traditions

---

[1] The letters of St Cyprian, Bishop of Carthage (ob. A.D. 258), give classic and relatively early expression to this conception of authority. To Antonianus (*ep.* 55) he writes: 'In reference, however, to the character of Novatian and to your written request for information as to his heresy, you must know first of all that we ought not even to be inquisitive as to what he teaches, so long as he is an outsider (nos primo in loco nec curiosos esse debere quid ille doceat, cum foris doceat). Whoever and whatsoever he may be, he is not a Christian who is not in the church of Christ (christianus non est qui in Christi ecclesia non est).' Cyprian goes on to define the church as 'one church divided by Christ throughout the whole world into many members, and one episcopate diffused throughout a harmonious multitude of many bishops (episcopatus unus episcoporum multorum concordi numerositate diffusus)'. To Florentius (*ep.* 66) he writes: 'You ought to know, therefore, that the bishop is in the church and the church is in the bishop (et ecclesiam in episcopo).' The letter to Jubaianus (*ep.* 73) contains the famous sentence, 'salus extra ecclesiam non est'.

It is pertinent to add that St Augustine (ob. A.D. 430) did not use the famous words which certain Roman apologists have put into his mouth at the time of the Pelagian controversy, 'Roma locuta est, causa finita est'. All that he says (*Sermo* 131) is that two councils were sent to the apostolic see whence came the rescripts settling the matter. 'Causa finita est; utinam aliquando finiatur error (the issue is settled; would that error were now at last at an end).'

of men'. But within Protestantism, too, an excessive logic has sometimes played havoc with this its constitutive principle; and the Bible, instead of being a living Word sounding out from God's historic revelation in Hebrew nation and Christian Church, has sometimes become a literally inerrant law-book. Calvin's great principle, 'scriptura duce et magistra', could degenerate into a narrow biblicism in the hands of later Calvinism. Indeed, such biblicism almost became bibliolatry in a Swiss confession of the seventeenth century, which declared that the Hebrew manuscript of the Old Testament was accepted as inspired of God not only in regard to the consonants, but also in regard to the vowel points.[1]

The third type may be loosely described as mystical. Stressing the inwardness not only of religious but also of all true authority, its constitutive principle is the 'Inner Light'. To quote the Quaker classic, Barclay's *Apology*: 'These divine inward revelations...are not to be subjected to the test either of the outward testimony of the Scriptures or of the natural reason of man...for this divine revelation and inward illumination is that which is evident and clear of itself' (Prop. ii). Here the danger of an excessive subjectivism is obvious; when each man's private fancies claim absolute authority in the name of direct, divine inspiration, the step from the Inner Light to the Outer Darkness is a small one. The danger to which such mysticism is always exposed lies in its undisciplined attitude to history; it is virtually indifferent to those outward forms (Book, Institutions, Sacraments, Ministry) which have been

---

[1] *Formula Consensus Ecclesiarum Helvetiarum Reformatarum* (1675), canon ii: 'accepimus hodieque retinemus, tum quoad consonas, tum quoad vocalia, sive puncta ipsa, sive punctorum saltem potestatem, et tum quoad res, tum quoad verba....'

and are the historic channels for the mediation of Christian truth. Mysticism often pays a heavy price for its tendency to belittle the historical and the factual. You will remember Gibbon's annihilating comment on the whirling dervishes of the desert: 'they mistook the giddiness of the head for the illumination of the Spirit.' After all, not only in science and art, but also in religion, the wisdom of the expert, distilled from the deposit of the past, has a definite authority which is not inconsistent with the responsibility of the individual for his own judgments.

There, then, are the three great types; and the history of Christendom too often shows them confronting one another like the three duellists in Sheridan's play *The Critic*, each aware of its ultimate logical incompatibility with the other two, and each fighting on two fronts. In point of fact, however, they are not so much different answers to the question about authority as answers revealing differences of emphasis. All three occupy the same common ground; for all three the Bible, the Church and personal faith are authoritative. In theory they are mutually exclusive, but in fact they interlock. Each exercises an interpretative control over the other two.

For example, all Christians believe in the Inner Light, 'the inward testimony of the Holy Spirit', to use the language of the Reformed tradition. The truth that God was in Christ reconciling the world unto himself is not truth for any man, be he Roman or Calvinist, until he makes it his own. But the Quaker does not discover what God has done for him on the Cross *in vacuo*, as it were. Without the witness of the Bible and the corroborative testimony of ecclesiastical experience and thought in every age, how could the fact of Christ have been mediated to him at all? Christian faith is rooted in the soil of history;

though personally appropriated it is nevertheless historically mediated.

Again, all Christians believe in the Bible as the Word of God. Roman dogma no less than Quaker piety makes this sufficiently plain. The mediaeval sermon, as Canon Charles Smyth has reminded us, was firmly anchored to the Bible.[1] Indeed, the plenary inspiration of Scripture is a dogma of the Roman Church.[2] But without the hearing ear and the response of faith this speech of God in Holy Scripture would remain a dead letter. Nor could individual Christians—a St Francis, a Luther or an Elizabeth Fry—have this personal experience for ever or for long without the divine society which has been its vehicle and guarantee in history. To use the well-known words of St Augustine, 'Indeed, I should not believe in the Gospel unless the authority of the catholic church aroused the belief in me'.[3]

Again, all Christians believe in the authority of their Holy Mother, the Church, in whose womb they have been conceived, at whose bosom they have been fed and by whose discipline they have been nurtured. This, so far from being a piece of legalistic dogmatism, is a spiritual fact. It is not a narrow legal injunction but a reality of history. Here, Cyprian in the third century and Calvin in the sixteenth, speak almost

[1] *The Art of Preaching*, p. 45. On the other hand see pp. 46 n. and 53 for ignorance of the Bible in the Middle Ages.

[2] Council of Trent, Session iv, April 1546: *Decretum de canonicis scripturis*. Also Vatican Council, Session iii, April 1870: *Constitutio dogmatica de fide catholica*, c. 2, *De revelatione*. The books of the Old and New Testaments (Vulgate edition) are revered as sacred because, written by inspiration of the Holy Spirit, they have God for their author (propterea quod Spiritu Sancto inspirante conscripti Deum habent auctorem).

[3] 'Ego vero evangelio non crederem, nisi me catholicae ecclesiae commoveret auctoritas' (*Contra epistolam quam vocant fundamenti*, c. 4).

precisely the same language.[1] Christians everywhere confess that the Church is an extension of the Incarnation. True Christian experience is always ecclesiastical experience. But this truth may not be made a cloak for any authoritarian position claimed in the name of new presbyter or old priest; moreover, what is true of priest and presbyter is also true of the 'priesthood of all believers', a precious scriptural principle which degenerates all too easily into an unscriptural egalitarian cliché.

Christian doctrine is the historic monument to the fact that God speaks and the soul hears, within the orbit of tradition represented by Scripture and the Church. These two authorities are organically one, in that they mediate the Word of the Gospel to men. The believer receives the Word by these channels only. But, as Karl Barth has insisted, the channels are no more than channels; neither is infallible in the sense that it is identical with the Word. The treasure is given to us in earthen vessels; through these means of grace the life-giving waters are offered to every one that thirsteth. But thirsty souls must come to the waters; not until it is heard is the Word effectually

---

[1] Calvin, *Institutio*, IV. i. 1, 4: 'Incipiam autem ab Ecclesia: in cuius sinum aggregari vult Deus filios suos, non modo ut eius cura etiam materna regantur donec adolescant, ac tandem perveniant ad fidei metam....Non alius est in vitam ingressus nisi nos ipsa concipiat in utero, nisi pariat, nisi nos alat suis uberibus, denique sub custodia et gubernatione sua nos tueatur....Haec enim quae Deus coniunxit separari fas non est, ut quibus ipse est Pater, Ecclesia etiam mater sit....Adde quod extra eius gremium nulla est speranda peccatorum remissio, nec ulla salus.'

Cf. Cyprian, *De catholicae ecclesiae unitate*, v, vi: 'Illius fetu nascimur, illius lacte nutrimur, spiritu eius animamur....Habere iam non potest Deum patrem, qui Ecclesiam non habet matrem.' But see also *Inst.* IV. viii. 13.

2-2

uttered; without man's full response of faith to God's Word mediated through the Bible and the holy catholic Church, the means of grace would be ineffectual and meaningless.

This familiar doctrine of three interlocking authorities—the three-fold operation of the Holy Spirit in the Bible, in the Church and in the soul of the individual believer—is admirably stated by Professor Dodd in a recent article on Revelation.[1] 'God reveals himself to us in Christ his Son, the eternal Word incarnate, through the testimony of the Scriptures and the interior testimony of the Holy Spirit. We receive his revelation by faith, which is itself the gift of God. We receive it in the context of the life of the Church, the Body of Christ, the custodian of the Scriptures, the dwelling place of the Holy Spirit. When in the fellowship of the Church we read the Scriptures, hear the Gospel of Christ proclaimed and partake in the Sacraments (the Eucharist in particular) we believe that God deals with us, and makes himself known to us as our Father, our Saviour and our Lord.'

The word Revelation brings us to a problem which may be introduced with a sharp question. What of human reason and its rights? Has it no part to play in the tremendous assertion that God is, and that men may know him? It is all very well for Christian doctrine to assert that the believer lives by revelation, and to claim that for him God is not Aristotle's Unmoved First Mover, the virtually unknown God of metaphysical speculation, but the God of Isaiah and the Psalmist, the God and Father of our Lord Jesus Christ. Does this mean that philosophical theology is a contradiction in terms and that the traditional intellectual discipline of the *philosophia*

[1] *Expository Times*, July 1940.

perennis can give us no knowledge of ultimate reality? Surely human reason has been and is a valid instrument of religious enquiry. 'The flight from reason', says Dr Prestige, 'marks the first stage in the surrender of religion to intellectual nihilism and vulgar superstition.'[1]

This burning modern issue is by no means new to the history of Christian doctrine. The nature of revelation must always be a crucial problem for a religion which finds its living heart in an Incarnation.

On the one hand, giants like Origen in the third century, Thomas Aquinas in the thirteenth and Richard Hooker in the sixteenth, vindicated the place of reason in their great theological systems. They were debtors, supremely to Holy Scripture of course, but also to Plato and Aristotle.

On the other hand, Tertullian in the early third century mocked at Aristotle, and in one of his most mischievous books argued that the search for truth was a confession of apostasy.[2] Bernard of Clairvaux in the twelfth century condemned the whole philosophic method in theology as 'disgraceful curiosity'.[3] Luther used language of characteristic extravagance in rejecting the notion of an autonomous human reason which is able of itself to apprehend the divine; to him reason was 'the devil's bride'. Like Barth,[4] four centuries later, he denied the very possibility of 'natural' theology. Kant, too, was in line with modern continental Protestantism in denying that man

[1] *Fathers and Heretics*, p. 136. This is timely, but it must be read in the light of the fine passage in defence of Christianity as a revealed religion on pp. 20–21.

[2] *De praescriptionibus haereticorum*, cc. x–xiv.

[3] 'turpis curiositas'. See Prestige, *op. cit.* p. 134 n.

[4] 'Es gibt kein menschliches Vorher', i.e. here there are no philosophical presuppositions.

can ever prove God's existence by the speculation of the intellect. His *Critique of Pure Reason* is a barrier set up between all attempted demonstrations of God's existence and true knowledge of God. Even Goethe, in his *Conversations with Eckermann*, observed emphatically that the Christian religion has nothing to do with philosophy.[1] And Ritschl, one of the greatest theologians of the nineteenth century, despised metaphysics almost to the point of pragmatism; indeed, he once made the profound and dangerous statement, 'without Christ I should be an atheist'. Such a list may fittingly end with James Denney's dry remark that one of the most serious difficulties to be contended with in a theological college is the divinity student who has previously obtained second-class honours in philosophy.

But, granted that Denney rightly deplored in a minister of religion a proud reluctance to accept God's revelation of himself in history, did he mean that the Christian man may never serve God with the mind? What, for example, of the traditional arguments for the existence of God, as set forth in varying forms by some of the greatest thinkers? Must one say that a rational demonstration of the existence of the living God is impossible, and that such speculation is never more than an attempt, as pathetic as it is heroic, to attain the unattainable?

At the risk of absurd over-simplification let me try to state the essential content and meaning of six of those arguments.

One of the oldest is labelled Cosmological, because it looks at

[1] 'Hegel zieht die christliche Religion in die Philosophie herein, die doch nichts darin zu thun hat. Die christliche Religion ist ein mächtiges Wesen für sich, woran die gesunkene und leidende Menschheit von Zeit zu Zeit sich immer wieder emporgearbeitet hat; und indem man ihr dieser Wirkung zugesteht, ist sie über aller Philosophie erhaben und bedarf von ihr keiner Stütze' (*Gespräche*, ii. 39).

the cosmos, the visible universe, and denies that it is self-explanatory. The natural order does not contain its complete explanation within itself, but points beyond itself. 'This goodly frame, the earth,...this most excellent canopy, the air,... this brave o'erhanging firmament, this majestical roof fretted with golden fire' presupposes a transcendent source or ground, an Ultimate Reality on which everything else depends, an *ens necessarium* which is the *ens realissimum*. Our very sense of temporality, change and decay has meaning only if the eternal and the unchanging is its background; we cannot confess that all our knowledge is relative without thereby betraying our belief in an Absolute which alone gives meaning and measure to relativity. Our knowledge of any event in nature is complete only when the full reason for that event is found in an Ultimate which is its own *raison d'être*, and which, because it does not depend on anything else, is not of nature but above it.[1]

In the second place, there is the ever-recurring argument labelled Teleological, which is abandoned only to be revised and restated, because its appeal is irresistible. Here we are concerned not with the origin and ground of all 'becoming', but with its purpose and end. Thinking men cannot believe that the many signs of design in nature are a sheer accident, having no ultimate significance. The universe seems orderly rather than disorderly, in that it is always realizing 'ends' which only an excessive scepticism will dismiss as meaningless. Confronted with nature's indubitable purposiveness at all its levels, man cannot believe that it is all 'spots and jumps', an unmeaning chaos. Is the whole process of organic evolution explicable to our human minds save on the hypothesis that

[1] See A. E. Taylor's remarkable chapter in *Essays Catholic and Critical*, entitled 'The Vindication of Religion', especially pp. 46–55.

such purposiveness implies not only Mind, but creative Mind, beyond all that is, yet working out its purposes within all that is?

In the third place, there is the argument which may be labelled Rational, because it reckons seriously with the authority of human reason and our inexpugnable conviction that this world is rational. The most significant fact about the whole evolutionary process is the evolution of mind which is able to know that process, to think about it and to evaluate it. The very possibility of science depends on the fact that nature answers to our thought about it, and that our thought answers to nature. Science has to assume as axiomatic the authority of reason and the self-consistency of reality. Obviously reason cannot prove its own authority. We cannot help believing, therefore, that the system which thus responds to mind is itself the work of Mind, a Mind which is infinite and universal and which influences and directs the evolutionary process throughout, because 'It' is transcendent and creative. Such a Mind cannot be contained within the universe. To explain man's mind and the authority of reason over it by saying that 'Nature' has produced his mind as the oyster produces the pearl, is to explain 'six' by saying that it is 'half-a-dozen'— which is no explanation at all. Why and how does nature come to have this capacity? Is any answer possible save that nature produces mind because it never was without Mind? The alpha and omega of all things, their beginning and their end, is the creative Thought of God. In different ages there are different standards of rationality, admittedly. But what matters here is not so much the varying standard of rationality as the fact of it. Our very repudiation of this or that as 'irrational', implies faith in its opposite; the negation logically involves an affirmation.

In the fourth place, there is the argument labelled Moral, because it springs from that consciousness of moral obligation in man which makes him *man* and differentiates him from termites, elephants and the most intelligent sheep-dogs that ever were. Man's distinctive and imperious sense of 'ought-ness' has a sanctity which refuses to be bargained with, or to be explained away in terms of any alien principle. The ancient Sophists who 'debunked' various institutions in the life of the Greek city-state, saying that these institutions were conventional (νόμῳ) rather than natural (φύσει), have perpetuated their memory in our word 'sophistry'. It is sophistry to argue that right and wrong have no foundation in the eternal order of things. The plain man's inescapable conviction that treachery, lies and lust are wrong, is not a socially begotten value-judgment, a useful human convention. His sense that mercy, truth and honour have eternal validity is no hedonistic calculus, subtly camouflaged, nor the unconscious rationalization of self-interest. Man cannot dismiss his sense of sacred obligation any more than he can escape from his shadow. The content of that felt obligation may vary from age to age, but the fact of it stands for ever, and its meaning is indubitable. As John Oman observes somewhere, 'whoever says "ought", really meaning "ought", is in that act bearing witness to the supernatural and supra-temporal as the destined home of man'. An obligation wholly independent of temporal consequences ('come rack, come rope') clearly cannot have its origin and justification in the temporal. Only to a being who has eternity in his heart,[1] because he is made in God's image, can the words 'Thou oughtest' have indestructible meaning. And if it be true that a moral ideal can exist only in a mind, an absolute moral ideal

[1] Eccles. iii. 11 (R.V. margin).

can exist only in a Mind which is the source and sustainer of all moral excellences, all reality.

In the fifth place, there is the argument labelled Ontological; it contends that the idea of God would not enter man's mind at all, unless man's being had its source and ground in him whose Being is wholly other than man's being and yet inclusive of it. The very idea of God is possible to us only because God already stands behind it. 'I believe', said Anselm, 'in order that I may understand.'[1] Human thought is always a signpost pointing to something beyond itself; deny this something, and all human thought is denied along with it. The mind of man is unintelligible unless Mind directs the whole creative process which has brought that mind to birth. On any other view it would be impossible to rely on the power of the mind to know truth. The ontological argument—always being shown out politely at the front door, but always quietly coming in again at the back, in a slightly different dress—is the affirmation of faith that belief in God is an absolute presupposition of all rational enquiry.

Lastly, there is the argument which might be labelled Human, because it springs out of the religious experiences and acts which, for all their bewildering variety, are integral to the history of humanity. Human history provides that basic religious experience to which the successive self-revelations of God make their appeal, and without which God's revelation in Jesus Christ would be impossible. The history of religion is not, in itself, revelation. Revelation is always more than religious experience. It is, to quote Paul Tillich,[2] the divine criticism and transformation of religious experience. Man's whole

[1] 'Credo ut intelligam' (*not* 'Intelligo ut credam').
[2] Dudleian Lecture (1935) on *Natural and Revealed Religion*.

26

religious history may not be explained as the mere outflow of his unique human nature. For man's nature is rooted in the mystery of his freedom to transcend his nature. It is this very freedom which is the basis of man's history. Our history is not determined by our nature; it is not the mere product of natural necessities; it is the creative context of God's living word to man.

The six arguments, stated here so baldly, have all played a vital role in the history of Christian doctrine. Their value lies in their cumulative testimony that God is. But *who* God is, God himself must tell us in revelation or we shall never know. Revelation means a dynamic self-disclosure on the part of the Other, to which man responds by faith. Man transcends his finiteness in the very act of being aware of his finiteness.

We ought to notice, in passing, that this response is not in principle peculiar to the religious man; it may not be dismissed as credulity which the natural sciences have outgrown. Faith is the presupposition of all discovery and of all progress in knowledge. Our most fundamental convictions—that we exist, or that the external world is no dream but really *there*— are not reached or proved by argument; they are given in experience. They may be defended by argument of course, but that is another matter. All men live by deep, inexorable intuitions, such as that of the plain man who trusts to common sense, that of the physicist who makes use of unprovable hypothesis,[1] and that of the religious man whose faith is response to revelation.

[1] 'The hypotheses of science are nothing more or less than explanations put forward to embrace a set of facts, or theories previously unrelated; and these hypotheses are not demonstrable in themselves. Such hypotheses as the force of gravity, space-time coincidences, the

This means, therefore, that revelation and response interpret one another. Divine self-disclosure is meaningless except in terms of human discovery, and *vice versa*. It means, further, that the great central tradition in Christian doctrine avoids two extreme views which are poles asunder in their mutual opposition.

The one view is represented by Spengler, whose dominant principle is a thorough-going relativism; he denies that there is any absolute truth for man. There is no revelation. Human convictions are always relative, one man's centre being another man's horizon. The search for absolute truth is like a fountain, striving to heaven and falling back in tears.

The other view is that of Karl Barth, who regards all natural theology as an attack on the absolute otherness and sole causality of God, and as no better than idolatry. Indeed, natural theology is a contradiction in terms. Revelation altogether transcends human philosophy; it occurs *in* the mind of regenerate man, but it comes from the Beyond, like a bolt from the blue. Its operation is exactly opposite to that of a fountain, in that it comes straight down from above (*senkrecht von oben*) in certain events, of which the Bible is the record. God's revelation is given; sinful man's passivity is complete; even the faith by which he responds to the sheer gift of God in Christ is altogether God's gift.

With the relativism and pessimism of Spengler's view, Christian doctrine can have nothing to do; the Bible is a

ether, the wave-theory of light, the general theory of relativity, are examples new and old of this kind of fruitful procedure which has not only connected seemingly random facts or theories, but lighted the way to the discovery of new and unsuspected facts' (Friend and Feibleman, *The Unlimited Community,* p. 183).

monument to the fact that the eternal God has never left himself without witness; its whole meaning is disclosed in the fact of the Incarnation; God has spoken to us in his Son.

What, on the other hand, must Christian doctrine say of the magnificent one-sidedness of Barth, whose theological transcendentalism has startled modern Christendom with its prophetic power and its indubitable desire to be loyal to the testimony of the Bible? Christian doctrine agrees that there is no experience of God without a revelation from God. Indeed, it insists with Barth that the God of natural theology is unable to give the religious certainty which is called forgiveness of sins, or grace; theism cannot give to sinful men a *saving* knowledge of God the Redeemer. But Christian doctrine asserts that divine revelation would be utterly impossible if there were no affinity or point of contact between man and God, no historical experience of the 'wholly Other', no capacity in unregenerate men to receive the sheer gift of grace. Man asks questions about God to which revelation is the answer; but the answer is intelligible only because the questions are intelligible. It is in this traffic between heaven and earth (Gen. xxviii. 11–19) that the divine revelation is given and received. Dreaming Jacob is not a mere cipher; his ladder is God's ladder; set up on earth, the top of it reached to heaven and the angels of God ascended and descended on it; and the Lord stood above it.

The problem of Revelation and Reason is to be understood, therefore, in terms of such a ladder rather than in terms of fountain or bolt from the blue. The Hebraic-Christian knowledge of the living God is always experience of the Object *in its relation to the subject*.[1] Since the Creator is altogether other than the creature, human experience of God's transcendent

[1] See further, ch. III.

otherness is plainly impossible. We do not know God as he is in himself; we know him only in his action and effect upon us; our very addressability is a fact of his appointing; our faith itself is his gift. To say that we love because he first loved us is to say that our love is the result which his initiative alone makes possible. Indeed, his effect upon us *is* our response. When St Paul insists that all is of God (Rom. xi. 36), he is drawing out the meaning of Christ's words to St Peter in Matt. xvi. 17. As often as Christ ends his teaching with the words 'he that hath ears to hear let him hear', he proclaims that the problem of Revelation and Reason is not a conundrum for man's intellect, but a demand made upon man's will by the infinite grace of God.

The fundamental question is this: How do we pass from abstract argument about God to living awareness of God? How have believing men found God, not as an inference from 'the starry world without and the moral law within', but as a living, saving God? Modern theology is returning to first principles in asking whether Christianity has its objective basis in moral idealism or in history. Is the Christian faith no more than a splendid illustration of the philosophy of moral values, or is it something given concretely in the events of time? Communism and Nazism are striking examples of the modern reaction against mere idealism, which is felt to be unrealistic and sentimental. Marx himself pointed men to facts, to the irresistible forces of history, not to the ineffectual aestheticism of value-judgments. Marx was a Jew, and although his debt to Hegel is obvious, his debt to the genius of Hebraism was more obvious than he realized.

For the Bible, which is Hebraic throughout, witnesses to

the holy will of God as purposive and continuously active in history. The Scriptures are not a philosophical treatise but a history book. The prophets did not believe in God because they deduced his existence from the facts of nature and history; on the contrary they brought a responsive belief in his revelation to the interpretation of nature and history.

After all, there is so much in nature and in history which is utterly inscrutable and mysterious to the boldest theistic speculation. It constitutes what we know as the problem of evil, a problem which is notoriously acute for all who believe in God. The Hebrew prophets, whose ethical monotheism towers above the common levels of history like a Himalaya range, were always wrestling with a two-fold mystery springing out of their faith that this is God's world and that man is the crown of God's creation. In the first place they had to wrestle with man's metaphysical distress at his own finitude and God's otherness. So far from always finding God in nature and history, they sometimes lost him there. 'Verily, thou art a God that hidest thyself.' The prophets speak for Everyman in witnessing to an irrational element in all religious experience. Like Rudolf Otto to-day, they reminded their generation that the meaning of human existence is not exhausted by the rational and the ethical; it escapes man's net and passes out into the ocean of ineffable mystery. In the second place, the prophets never ceased to wrestle with man's moral distress, the fact of sin in this world which God made and saw to be 'very good'—the dark, abiding, universal mystery of iniquity.

Thus, Scripture is less concerned with the philosophy of theism than with God's active and purposive revelation of himself as a living God and a Saviour. God himself makes answer to man's tragic estrangement from him. He, the

Creator and Sustainer of all that is, is the Holy One of Israel, working out the eternal purpose of his creation in judgment and mercy. He draws nigh to his world, mighty to save.

The Christian doctrine of creation does not arise from our interest in explaining the world or accounting for its 'origin' at some approximately dateable time in the cosmic past. The doctrine of creation 'out of nothing' is not a scientific description of the beginning of the time series. Here, no scientific statements are possible. 'Before Abraham was, I am' (John viii. 58). Belief in the creation means a way, *the* way, of understanding the present world. It is an act of faith (Hebr. xi. 3). Creation out of nothing is not to be understood as an historical event but as a description of existence. Here is truth which we receive by faith; we do not conceive it at all, since it transcends the utmost limit of all human conceiving. The doctrine of creation out of nothing is not a cosmological theory, but an expression of our adoring sense of the transcendent majesty of God and of our utter dependence upon him. The doctrine has a three-fold distinction.

In the first place it is distinguished from Deism, which isolates God from his universe and knows nothing about him except that he is the First Cause of all that is. The deist conceives of creation as a past act, the universe being like a wound-up clock working unaided by God, who exists in transcendent loneliness and inaccessibility. The Christian doctrine of creation, on the other hand, asserts that the transcendent God creates *in continuo actu*; i.e. he sustains the universe in every moment of its existence.

In the second place it is distinguished from Pantheism, which takes many forms and either resolves the whole universe into God or equates God with the universe. The whole of things is

God (the relation being one of identity, correlation or continuity); the world is the necessary self-unfolding of God, a divine emanation. The result is that God is depersonalized and lost. The World Soul of Pantheism is as abstract and unknowable as the First Cause of Deism. The Christian doctrine of creation through God's Word is a way of asserting that the Ultimate Reality is personal, creation being the free act of God's will and the continuous expression of his purpose.

In the third place it is distinguished from Dualism, which conceives of the universe as being formed out of a primal material, independent of God and in some sense hostile to him. According to Dualism God is the principle of Form battling against formless chaos; or he is Spirit warring against Matter in all its gross intractability. Christian doctrine repudiates all such forms of metaphysical dualism, by affirming that the universe is created by God alone 'out of nothing'; and that all things, though definitely distinct from him, are utterly dependent on him.

But the Christian doctrine of God the Creator cannot be adequately interpreted by the formal definitions of systematic theology; at any rate, a lecture on the living God should end, not with technical terminology but with the language of the heart. The living God is best interpreted by living men who have known him experimentally. One such man, George Fox, has told us in his journal what happened to him in Nottinghamshire in 1648: 'And one morning as I was sitting by the fire a great cloud came over me and a temptation beset me; but I sate still. And it was said: "All things come by nature"; and the elements and stars came over me, so that I was in a manner quite clouded with it.... And as I sate still under it, and let it alone, a living hope arose in me, and a true voice which said

"There is a living God who made all things". And immediately the cloud and temptation vanished away and life rose over it all; my heart was glad and I praised the living God. After some time I met with some people who had such a notion that there was no God, but that all things come by nature. I had a great dispute with them and overturned them and made some of them confess that there is a living God. Then I saw that it was good that I had gone through that exercise.'

II

MAN AND HIS SIN

THE CHRISTIAN DOCTRINE OF THE FALL

WHAT is the truth about the nature and end of man? This is the ultimate question behind the vast debate, the desperate struggles, of our time. Ideologies—to use the ugly modern jargon—are really anthropologies; they are answers to that question which man has not ceased to ask ever since he began asking questions at all; namely, What is Man? He asks this question about himself, because all his questions about the universe involve it. Who is the being who asks the questions?

We ought to notice at the outset that Christian doctrine decisively repudiates two classic attitudes towards this problem; two estimates of human nature and human history which have never lacked their defenders, and which are poles apart from one another. I mean, on the one hand, a naïve optimism; and, on the other hand, a cynical pessimism. Let us look at them in turn.

It is common form to-day to dismiss most forms of liberalism—in sociology, politics and theology, for example—as unrealistic and sentimental. To quote a mordant paragraph which T. E. Hulme wrote about moral idealism twenty-four years ago: 'it is as if you pointed out to an old lady at a garden party that there was an escaped lion twenty yards off, and she were to reply, "Oh, yes," and then quietly take another cucumber sandwich.'

In short, realism is in the ascendant, as a multitude of writers remind us; in the face of stubborn realities, the complacency of mere idealism is as nauseating as its moral inadequacy. Modern man is suffering from disillusionment, now that the evolutionary optimism of half a century ago is plainly discredited by facts. Even in America the romantic illusions of Utopianism are an ebbing tide, as the mystery of iniquity is seen to be a real and an abiding mystery: not something exceptional, a bad patch which a young civilization like that of the United States will soon mop up, but something typical of all civilizations: not the surface blemish which education, modern science, low-price technics and three-piece plumbing will rectify, but a deep-seated radical evil which is uncomfortably reminiscent of what Jonathan Edwards knew as original sin. The Americans are not as sure as they were that sin is only an 'evolutionary overhang'. They are no longer confident that what has been called the sin-obsession of Christianity is just so much 'crêpe-hanging'.

'We were getting richer, more numerous, busier, every year', says Professor Adams of the Capitalist era which arrived overnight in 1850. 'Back in the East, Hermann Melville had written an American classic, *Moby Dick*; but no one knew or cared what the White Whale signified or whether there was any evil in the Universe. We preferred Emerson, who asked us to be cultured and spiritual, and hopefully looked like the rest of us for spirit to evolve somehow out of matter; and blessed our railroads to a divine use. But the dark cloud in the American sky grew blacker and was spreading.'[1]

---

[1] *The Epic of America*, p. 234.

The fact is that our generation is rediscovering the abysmal depths of evil in the heart of man, and realizing that Public Enemy Number One is neither ignorance, nor stupidity, nor the defective social environment, but *sin*, which is the deep mysterious root of all these evils.

To be explicit, Christian doctrine brings a three-fold count against the confident optimism of modern civilization.

First, the root error of Utopian idealism is its failure to take a sufficiently tragic view of human nature. It blandly assumes the natural and fundamental goodness of man, shutting its eyes to the fact that under sufficient stress the modern man— not to mention the modern woman—will do deeds of evil as terrible as anything recorded in history.

Christianity's second count against the Utopian humanism of our time is that it clings to that peculiarly modern superstition, man's perfectibility and his inevitable progress. Granted, it says, that darkness covereth the earth and gross darkness the peoples, still, we shall ultimately achieve control over the demonic, irrational, and savage forces, which have, admittedly, tried men's faith and broken their hearts in every generation until now. Sin must not become an obsession, therefore. We need not take it too seriously. As some wag observed about the adolescence of the Quaker, George Fox, 'he had sown his wild oats, but they were only Quaker Oats'. That is, he grew out of his youthful difficulties and humanity will do the same.

The answer to this dogma of human perfectibility is that history does not disclose so neat and simple a pattern. There is a tragic antinomy in the whole world process, to which Christ himself bears witness in the parable of the Wheat and the Tares. They grow together until history reaches its climax of ultimate judgment; the New Testament knows nothing of history as the record of human progress wherein evil is steadily conquered by good. And we know nothing of it either. History is the record of 'an ever-increasing cosmos creating ever-increasing possibilities of chaos';[1] in other words, as our state of civilization makes progress, so the difficulties and dangers which keep it company make progress too. At every instant these difficulties and dangers bear a nearly constant ratio to the state of civilization which we have reached. Do the facts suggest that with our enormously extended mastery of nature, there goes a corresponding mastery of our evil wills, our lusts, our hypocrisies, our boundless egotisms—above all, our fears? They do not. The light of progress is real; granted. But the new dangers and degradations which are its accompanying shadow are also real. Along with the internal combustion engine there comes slaughter on the roads: along with aviation, bombs. Chemical research in the interests of medicine brings with it phosgene and vesicant dew, mustard gas and arsene. The education which was to have banished crime, only makes crime more efficient, increasing its range. Man's power to do more good is always power to do more evil. Chateaubriand, nourished like many a young Frenchman at the time of the French Revolution on legends of America, was surprised on landing there to be met at a farmyard gate by a negro girl, thirteen years old. 'We bought maize-cakes, chickens, eggs and milk and went abroad again with our baskets. I gave my silk handkerchief to the little African girl. It was a slave who welcomed me to the Land of Liberty.'[2]

But this is not all. Christian doctrine makes yet a third count against the optimistic estimate of human nature. Long

[1] Reinhold Niebuhr, *An Interpretation of Christian Ethics*, p. 108.
[2] André Maurois, *Chateaubriand*, p. 48.

before the advent of modern psycho-analysis, Christian doctrine had unmasked much that passes for righteousness and high moral principle. It had insisted that there is no sin so subtle as the sin of 'goodness', as popularly or legalistically conceived. 'And he spake this parable unto certain which trusted in themselves that they were righteous....Two men went up into the temple to pray; the one a Pharisee, and the other a publican. The Pharisee stood and prayed thus with himself, God, I thank thee, that I am not as other men are, extortioners, unjust, adulterers, or even as this publican....And the publican, standing afar off, would not lift up so much as his eyes unto heaven, but smote upon his breast, saying, God be merciful to me a sinner. I tell you, this man went down to his house justified rather than the other' (Luke xviii. 9–14). Righteousness so easily cloaks the sin of self-righteousness. There is no sin so subtly dangerous as the self-sufficiency of the morally religious man. Indeed, all our righteousness is tainted. High-sounding moral principles often include a rationalization of our self-interest. Is it not fatally easy for a class or a nation to be blind to the ways in which its interests condition its moral pronouncements? The egotism of the will to power asserts itself not as egotism of course, but as an idealism of some kind or other. Modern Imperialism is the white man's burden. Modern Communism is a crusade for social righteousness. The militarist almost always regards modern war as a just war; the pacifist almost always interprets his objection to its evil and misery as a matter of conscience. Such high claims to disinterestedness are doubtless sincere, yet it may be doubted whether they are always an exhaustive account of what they would describe. We readily acknowledge that Satan appears as an angel of light, but we are less ready to see that all culture, including religious culture, is tainted with the same hypocrisy. Corruption touches even this. Even at its best, man's goodness is poisoned; there is this canker or flaw in it, so that it actually becomes a barrier to his reconciliation with God. The whole of the New Testament contrast between grace and works is bound up with this fact. It is fatally easy for a man to use his moral rectitude to veil the proud egocentricity which it supremely illustrates. This is the Christian version of the Greek ὕβρις. The self-sufficiency of the morally religious man is itself the full measure of sin. We come to understand the great word 'Grace' only when we perceive that this legalistic relation to God is itself sin. The parable of the Prodigal Son is an immortal illustration of this attempt to do business with God as though he were not the Holy Father but a banker keeping a debit and credit account with us. The attitude of both the sons was commercial. The younger son wanted an overdraft: the elder brother wanted to open a deposit account.[1] And the latter is sin at its deepest and deadliest.

To sum up: or, rather, to let Browning's well-known lines sum up the realism of the Christian faith:

> 'Tis the faith that launched point-blank its dart
> At the head of a lie; taught Original Sin,
> The corruption of man's heart.

Great thinkers of modern times, Montaigne and Pascal, Bunyan and Kierkegaard, Nietzsche and Sigmund Freud, have probed the human heart and told the truth about its strength. Their analysis only confirms the radical realism of the Biblical view of man. The congenital weakness of human nature is the submerged rock on which the complacent claims of an opti-

---

[1] Professor T. W. Manson's epigram.

mistic humanism are shipwrecked. Indeed, as Professor Hodges of Reading pointed out in a News-Letter some months back,[1] the gospel that good-will is the one thing needful is so clearly false, that people who see its falsehood have been driven away from Christianity because they have been led to think that this is Christian doctrine.

But, now, in the second place, Christian doctrine repudiates a cynical pessimism with equal decisiveness. Pessimism, if it be real and thorough, is as unchristian as an excessive optimism. Thorough-going despair is pagan. To despair of man is not unchristian—far from it. But to despair of man in such a way that you are really despairing of God is blasphemy. Indeed, it is atheism.

Thomas Hobbes, significantly enough, was charged with atheism. And atheism is implicit in his assertion of the utter self-centredness and lovelessness of man. According to Hobbes human life without the control of the totalitarian state at every point would be 'solitary, poor, nasty, brutish and short'. Hobbes had no real belief in the redeeming grace of God; he believed in Leviathan.

This view finds its exponents to-day. If the optimists (Social Democrats and others) have affirmed that the function of the state is to make a Utopia of human society, the sole function of the state according to the pessimists is to prevent human society from becoming Hell. Indeed, more than one continental theologian takes a very similar view, notably Gogarten.

All this inevitably raises an obvious question which may best be dealt with at this point. What are we to make of the grim and terrible doctrine of Total Corruption—found in Holy Scripture

[1] *Christian News-Letter*, Supp. No. 27.

certainly, but worked out with an unscriptural and pitiless logic by St Augustine and the Reformers? Man is 'utterly leprous and unclean'. If this is not blasphemous pessimism, what is? What did it mean?

Well, if it meant what a classic statement of it seems to mean when taken out of its historic context and interpreted literally, namely, that we 'are utterly indisposed, disabled and made opposite to all good, and wholly inclined to all evil' (*West. Conf.* vi. 4), it is plainly indefensible. If Total Corruption meant that every man is as bad as he can be, it would be totally absurd, simply because the conception is self-destroying, as Professor John Baillie has reminded us.[1] 'A totally corrupt being would be as incapable of sin as would a totally illogical being of fallacious argument.' But, in spite of the deplorable extravagance of the language of some Reformers here, notably Luther, this doctrine of Total Corruption was really insisting that the depravity which sin has produced in human nature *extends to the whole of it*, permeates human life and experience *in all its ranges*; that there is no part of man's nature, *not even his virtue*, which is unaffected by it. Total Corruption does not and never did mean that the stream of human history, instead of being crystal clear, is solid mud; but that it is impure, corrupted in every part of its course; that even the purest ideals and the most disinterested achievements of individuals and societies are, as we have already seen, tainted by sinful self-interest and pride. Human justice is itself proof of this, since anything short of love as revealed in Christ cannot be perfect justice. Perfect justice would be love. As Niebuhr has remarked, 'Love is the only final structure of freedom'. But our justice—our prisons and cash-registers, our private property, our elaborate

[1] *Our Knowledge of God*, p. 33.

42

devices for checking one another and our signatures on the dotted line—all this is a monument to the radical and abiding wrongness of humanity, as measured by the absolute norm of love.

The Reformers knew that if you look at human virtue and merit, not from the ethical but from the strictly theocentric standpoint, all righteousness is as filthy rags. There is none righteous, no not one. They said so. They meant that fallen and rebellious man is utterly impotent to come unaided to that saving knowledge of God for which he was created. He cannot bring his state into harmony with his true nature. He cannot fulfil the destiny for which he was created in the image of God. 'Thou must save, and thou alone.' The doctrine of Total Corruption was the intransigent answer which Reformation theology made to Renaissance Humanism. But to suppose, therefore, that the Reformers were antinomian, and that they had no interest in ethics, is nonsense. They recognized that, ethically considered, man is a mixture of good and evil, and that men's sins differ in degree as well as in direction. They were not blind to what the New Testament has to say about human conduct which is relatively good; about men's moral growth; about extenuating circumstances which make human guilt a matter of degree. Indeed, they had a Puritan horror of lawlessness and fully recognized man's positive achievements for good in the arts and sciences, and in politics. But they knew that such cultural values—admittedly excellent in themselves—are unable to answer the deepest longings of the soul of man; culture gives no answer to the question of the ages, 'What must I do to be saved?' In short, theirs was neither the easy optimism of the humanist, nor the dark pessimism of the cynic, but the radical realism of the Bible. Mere pessimism would be a poor and pagan answer to a sentimental and irreligious optimism. It is an answer which Christian anthropology has never given, so long as it has remained true to its own first principles.

What are those principles? We are now in a position to state them, albeit summarily.

The first principle of Christian anthropology is that man, like the animals, is God's creature. Though he is God's last and highest earthly creature, his creatureliness is an inescapable and abiding fact. But, unlike the animals, man is more than a natural creature. He is lifted above all other earthly creatures in being made in the image of God, and in being aware of the fact. He is aware that the Creator is the Eternal Love who calls men into existence that their willing response to his love may fulfil his creative purpose. This responsible awareness which God created in man (*Ansprechbarkeit*, addressability, or answerability, as Brunner has called it) is man's greatness and his fatal temptation. As Brunner observes,[1] this responsibility or addressability was not a task, but a gift; not law, but grace. The Word, through which and in which man has his distinctive existence, was not an imperative of the divine law, but an indicative of the divine love. Man's 'Yes' was to be a response, not to 'Thou shalt', but to 'I have created and called thee; thou art mine'. Created in God's image, man was meant to be a son, not a bondservant under a law. There, then, is the first of the three fundamental principles of Christian anthropology. Man is a creature divinely endowed with gifts which set him above all other creatures; he is made in the image of God. It is impossible to understand man's fundamental disharmony and

[1] *Man in Revolt*, p. 98.

44

the immemorial misdirection of human life apart from this relationship of man to the Creator who made him in his own image.

The second principle witnesses to the universal fact of man's rebellious estrangement from God. Unlike the animals man is a sinner: he falls below all earthly creatures in his rebellious denial of a responsibility which they can never know.

The essence of sin is man's self-centred denial of his distinctive endowment. Its final ground is pride which rebels against God and repudiates his purpose. Its active manifestation is self-love which 'changes the glory of the incorruptible God into the image of the corruptible man'. The freedom of the filial spirit, man's freedom *for* God and *in* God, is perverted to mean freedom *from* God. *Imago Dei* is interpreted to mean 'Ye shall be as gods'. It is interesting and significant that in his last book the well-known psychologist, Jung, should describe man's proud trust in himself as 'his Godalmightiness'.[1]

The result is two-fold. First, alienation from God, as two immortal stories in Holy Scripture remind us: the story of the Garden of Eden, and the parable of the Prodigal Son. Man is not at home in his Father's house, but a needy outcast in a far country. Second, the wrath of God, which is the terrible way this alienation works out, both for the individual and in society. For man, though a sinner, remains God's creature. The prodigal among the husks is still a son: he does not become like one of Circe's swine. His initial endowment is indestructible. An animal, just because it is an animal, is unable to rebel against its endowment. And man, just because he is man, is unable to destroy his endowment. God's image is not destroyed.

[1] J. C. Jung, *The Integration of the Personality*, cited by Dr J. H. Oldham, *Christian News-Letter*, No. 36.

Sin always presupposes that which it defaces. 'Man could not be godless without God.'[1] And the form in which rebellious and fallen man experiences the eternal love of God is Wrath. His responsibility to God ceases to be a formula of his created being and becomes a formula of obligation. Liberty becomes bondage. This is 'the curse of the Law', that the will of God which it announces as the law of man's being is no longer a gift of life and the most natural thing in the world, but a death-bringing demand. It is all the difference between living at home, and being in prison. This is the second great principle of Christian anthropology.

The third principle witnesses to man's solidarity in evil. The word 'sin' has an individual reference, plainly enough: it is always a conscious and responsible act of will on the part of an individual. Yet this cannot be an exhaustive definition of it. Sin is also a state or condition of sinfulness mysteriously constitutive of our empirical make-up. It is never a man's private affair. Your failure matches mine and our lives interlock to form an organic system of evil. Indeed, St Augustine used the words 'sinful mass' (*massa peccatrix*) to describe this solidary aspect of human sin. Schleiermacher, too, described it as 'in each the work of all: in all the work of each'.[2] Dostoievsky reminds us that the solidarity of the race is a fact and, in view of the reality of sin, a terrible fact; 'we are each responsible to all for all'. The work which psychologists are now doing on the 'collective unconscious' goes to show that below not only the conscious, but also the unconscious life of the individual, there is a deep layer (as it were) of hidden, inborn forces: its content is not individual but universal and, as such, beyond the conscious control of the will. In speaking thus, psychology is only

[1] Brunner, *op. cit.* p. 187.　　　　[2] *Glaubenslehre*, § 71. 2.

confirming the witness of the New Testament, that humanity is subject to a possession or infection by evil from which no individual can dissociate himself. This possession is so sinister, cunning and strong that the New Testament can only describe it in terms of demonic powers. The personification of evil as Satan, difficult though it is for our thought, stands for the fact of spiritual solidarity in evil which will not be evaded or ignored. An enemy hath done this—our common Enemy![1] Whatever images of thought we may employ, there is in the world of our experience a kingdom of evil by which the evil acts of each individual are inspired, sustained and reinforced.

So far, then, we have been considering the first principles of the Christian doctrine of man and his sin.

The question now confronting us is obvious: Can sin be accounted for? According to a widespread modern view, brilliantly expounded by Tennant,[2] sin is explicable as an evolutionary survival from man's animal origin. Sin is our conscious misuse of impulses and instinctive passions which are part of our animal inheritance. In themselves these primary incentives to sin are neutral and non-moral. Indeed, they are not only biologically but morally necessary to our growth as men: they are the raw material of our moral life, and as much the condition and occasion of virtue as of vice. Animals can neither sin nor achieve sainthood; man, as a responsible moral

[1]   'Ich bin der Geist, der stets verneint....
         So ist denn alles was ihr Sünde,
         Zerstörung, kurz das Böse nennt,
         Mein eigentliches Element.'
                              Mephistopheles (*Faust*, 1).
[2] In *The Origin and Propagation of Sin* (1903) and *The Concept of Sin* (1912).

agent, can and does. His inborn conative tendencies are morally neutral, but his will which shapes and uses them is not. The will may be good or evil and as such it alone calls for moral approval or disapproval. Thus propensities not in themselves sinful are the condition and the explanation of sin's emergence when responsible man is evolved from the irresponsible animal.

Three criticisms of this view suggest themselves at once. First, we meet the old and tragic question: Why is sin universal? Even if we admit that this evolutionary theory describes *how* sin happens, why does it happen always and everywhere? How are we to account for that bias or perversion of the human will which makes sin an empirically universal fact and therefore virtually inevitable? As the very condition of moral action man must be free to choose the evil: but why is it that all men without exception do so, unless a sinful tendency is somehow part of their very nature? All serious thought about the mystery of iniquity has had to grapple with this its constitutional, as well as its volitional, aspect.

Many of our modern difficulties with regard to this problem spring from theological terms which hinder rather than help us. It cannot be stated too emphatically that 'Original Sin' neither implies nor means 'Original Guilt'. The latter expression carries with it forensic and penal implications which outrage the moral sense. No man may be judged guilty because of the misdeeds of his ancestor. Such a judgment would destroy the very meaning of morality. Therefore, such terminology which is only a stumbling-block to-day is better abandoned. But the empirical fact of universal evil (what Kant called *das radikale Böse*) remains, and whether or not we describe it as 'Original Sin', it demands some adequate description.

We must abandon the classical doctrine of Original Sin where it is bound up with the morally insupportable doctrine of Original Guilt, but we are still left with the historical fact of universal moral imperfection, whose reality that grim doctrine attested. As Edwyn Bevan has observed: 'When people say that man is naturally good or that his good and bad impulses are pretty evenly matched, how is it that all over the world to follow the good impulses has seemed like going uphill, and to follow the evil ones like going downhill?'[1] To explain this by appealing to the chronological priority of impulse to conscience, is only to carry the problem one stage further back and to leave it unexplained. Why are men such that conscience is always and everywhere outmatched? This is the fundamental and universal mystery which cries out for explanation.

In the second place, since sin necessarily implies guilt, how are we to explain it, that is, determine its causes, without *eo ipso* explaining its guilt away? Sin, like freedom, is by hypothesis inexplicable, since moral action presupposes freedom in the sense of real choice. Personal responsibility and freedom are the essence of what we mean by moral personality. But, if man is free no scientific formula can possibly cover the universality of sin, without taking away the element of responsibility which makes it what it is. Any alleged explanation of the fact that all men sin is only a new determinism.[2] If sin, universal as it is, is to be treated as a moral fact and not as a natural fact (such as the secretion of the bile) it must remain inexplicable. Determine

---

[1] *Symbolism and Belief*, p. 63.

[2] See H. W. Robinson, *The Christian Doctrine of Man* (second edition); the Appendix entitled 'Recent Thought on the Doctrine of Sin', pp. 353–4.

the causes of a universal moral fact and it ceases to be moral. It becomes natural, and is no more patient of moral evaluation than is gravitation or the beating of the heart or death. The attempt to trace sin back to an empirical fact which causes it, invalidates man's God-given sense that he is a will and a person. The will is *ex hypothesi* that which is non-derivable.[1] Man's sinful will cannot be explained: it must remain as the one completely irrational fact in a world which God created, and saw to be 'very good'.

The third difficulty here, on which von Hügel lays his sensitive finger, is that the permanent wound in man's nature which needs healing is deeper than anything biology can explain. The central, typical, fatal sin is self-sufficiency or pride. In the Christian view pride or self-love is the specific *differentia* of sin. The evolutionary hypothesis makes pride and self-sufficiency depend as truly upon our animal descent, as do gluttony or sloth. But, as von Hügel rightly observes, 'this single derivation will simply not work....Impurity may be the viler sin, but even impurity is instinctively felt here to be less deadly than pride.... Whilst impurity is occasioned by the body, pride is not; the doctrine of the Fall of the Angels grandly illustrates this deep instinct.'[2]

After all, the fundamental instinct of the animal world is the will to survive. Man's sin cannot be so explained, because it cannot be so described. It is the will to power which differentiates man from the animals, and constitutes the tragic dissidences of human history. Selfishness measures the inexplicable tragedy of the world. Man's proud unwillingness to

[1] 'das was nicht abgeleitet werden kann' (Paul Althaus, *Grundriss der Dogmatik*, ii. 66).

[2] *Essays and Addresses on the Philosophy of Religion* (1921), pp. 8–9.

accept the absolute authority and claim of God in whose image
he has been made, is and remains the mystery of iniquity.

What, then, of the doctrine of the Fall? Serious thought
about sin involves an irresolvable antinomy. As a universal
fact of human experience it is virtually unavoidable. As a
moral fact it is a matter of personal decision and responsibility.
Or, to put it another way: sin is rooted in man's inmost disposition; yet it is indubitably that for which his will is responsible. We face this fundamental problem therefore: how
are we to express the idea of *un*-freedom without laying ourselves open to the danger of determinism?[1]

Christian doctrine has attempted to do so in terms of man's
original state and the Fall, but it has sometimes defeated its
own intention by treating as literal history what can only be
a mythological framework. Christian doctrine illustrates the
fatal difficulty of trying to construct a history of sin out of the
concept of its inevitability. Luther's extravagant description
of the perfections of man's primitive state is as fantastic as
South's sermon on 'Man created in God's Image', which
contained the famous sentence: 'An Aristotle was but the
rubbish of an Adam, and Athens but the rudiments of
Paradise.'

The difficulty is two-fold. First, the victory of the sciences,
palaeontology and biology, shatters this picture as history.
Second, the Adam story is the main source of that determinism which the classic anthropology of Christendom hardly
avoids.

The idea of a Fall from an original state of perfection is

[1] Cf. Calvin, *Institutio* (1536), c. ii, *De Fide*: 'difficilis et involuta
quaestio: an Deus autor sit peccati.'

4-2

really a limiting conception, a theological *Grenzbegriff*. It is not a scientific statement about the dawn of history. The Fall is symbolism, necessary to the intellect, but inconceivable by the imagination.[1] It involves no scientific description of absolute beginnings. Eden is on no map, and Adam's fall fits no historical calendar. Moses is not nearer to the Fall than we are, because he lived three thousand years before our time. The Fall refers not to some datable aboriginal calamity in the historic past of humanity, but to a dimension of human experience which is always present—namely, that we who have been created for fellowship with God repudiate it continually; and that the whole of mankind does this along with us. Everyman is his own 'Adam', and all men are solidarily 'Adam'. Thus, Paradise before the Fall, the *status perfectionis*, is not a period of history, but our 'memory' of a divinely intended quality of life, given to us along with our consciousness of guilt. It is, to quote Paul Althaus, 'nicht historischer sondern wesentlicher Art';[2] that is, it describes the quality rather than the history of 'man's first disobedience'.

Man's tragic apostasy from God is not something which happened once for all a long time ago. It is true in every moment of existence. If you believe in the Creation, you must go on to believe in the Fall. The symbolism of the one is a necessary complement to the symbolism of the other.

Christian anthropology affirms the notorious conflict between man's recalcitrant will, and that divine purpose in which

---

[1] Speaking of self-transcendence, Auguste Lecerf writes: 'cette image, irréalisable pour l'imagination, est en quelque sorte nécessaire pour l'intelligence' (*De la Nature de la Connaissance Religieuse*, p. 291). This is an apt comment on all theological symbolism.

[2] *Op. cit.* p. 67.

alone man and his world find their true meaning. It describes that age-long misdirection of human life which is the very presupposition of the Gospel. Any other presupposition would make the glorious gospel of the blessed God meaningless.

A second Adam to the fight,
And to the rescue came.

III

THE KINGDOM OF GOD

THE CHRISTIAN DOCTRINE OF HISTORY

W E are near enough to our schooldays to remember
Macaulay's flattering but irritating references to
what 'every schoolboy knows'. These blandishments
deceived none of us, of course: we knew that by 'schoolboy'
he really meant Thomas Babington Macaulay.

Had I the nerve to begin this lecture by saying that every
schoolboy knows the difference between the Greek and Hebrew
ways of thinking about God I should merely mean that there
are few things more familiar to students of theology, or more
fundamental to the understanding of Christian doctrine.

It is easy to make foolish generalizations here, and to
exaggerate this well-known difference between Hellenism and
Hebraism. But the difference is real. It turns on the meaning
of history, and its relation to the eternal God, who is above
history. Let me try to express the difference in four ways.

First of all, the Greek and the Hebrew thought differently
about God's nature. To the Greek mind God is impersonal,
rather like an all-pervasive ether; an Absolute transcending
all differences; almost a complete Blank. The Ultimate Reality
is the One, who is one and all alone and ever more shall be so.
To the Hebrew, on the other hand, the Ultimate Reality is
personal; a living God. God is certainly one and transcendent
for the Hebrew mind, too; the Creator is eternally distinct

from his creation. But, as personal, righteous Will, he who is 'wholly other' is nevertheless very near to men.

In the second place, the Greek and the Hebrew thought differently about the way God is known. For the Greek, such knowledge is analogous to seeing; like looking at a distant landscape, for example. The knower is always at a distance from that which he would know. Contemplating the motionless, self-contained calm of Eternal Reality, he is not unlike a camera, photographing the most distant fixed star, millions of light-years away. His attitude is necessarily aesthetic. I mean that he is an observer and no more. There can be no relationship between knower and Known. Any communication across the separating abyss is unthinkable. Indeed it would be a disturbance, just as a photograph would be disturbed and spoiled by a movement of the Object, to say nothing of some clumsy movement on the part of the camera.

For the Hebrew, on the other hand, the knowledge of God comes to man by just such a movement, from the Beyond. For him, knowing God is analogous to hearing and answering. What is known is not the Object in itself, of course, but the Object in its action and effect on the knowing subject. God is known because his self-revealing Word is heard by an Isaiah or a Jeremiah, in and through the stuff of human history. Here is a living God whom to know is to obey. This is no mere aestheticism. Here, not only the intelligence but the will is involved. Deep calleth unto deep. It is no accident that after St Paul, the Hebrew, had seen a vision on the Damascus road, he could say, 'I was not disobedient unto the heavenly vision'. Only a Hebrew would talk of obeying a vision.

In the third place, the Greek and the Hebrew thought very differently about history. To the Greek, the time-process had no ultimate value. Nothing real ever moves. The glittering tumult of history in all its multiplicity, waywardness and concreteness is only a breaking wave on the ocean of Absolute Being. The wise man, said the Stoic, is not concerned with time.

But, to the Hebrew, time is God's creation and the workshop of his holy purpose. History is the arena wherein his will expresses itself as action. Revelation means that the acts and facts of history mediate and disclose the mighty acts of God. In short, to the Greek, history is not much more than a symbol: to the Hebrew, it is the instrument of the eternal God; the roaring loom on which the garment of his kingly rule is woven.

In the fourth place, Greek and Hebrew used what one might call different theological methods. Whereas intellectual speculation is the method of the Greek philosopher, the Hebrew prophet is not interested in it. His function is testimony. The prophets never ask whether God exists, nor do they infer his existence from the facts of nature. They witness, not even to the idea of God, but to God himself as morally and redeemingly active amid the movement of events. The Bible does not provide philosophical arguments for theism; it is a history book, witnessing to successive 'moments' in the creative and redemptive activity of God. Here, *Geschichte* is seen as *Heilsgeschichte*; that is, secular history is seen in terms of a framework of sacred history, which began in Paradise and will end in the New Jerusalem, where the Kingdom of God will find its victorious consummation, beyond time and death and corruption. Thus, the Christian doctrine of History is itself a history, a story rather than any abstract theory: it is, to quote the familiar hymn, 'the old, old story, of Jesus and his love'.

Since our immediate interest is theology, we have to join in this debate which is by no means peculiar to the ancient world of Athens and Jerusalem. This is no mere hobby-horse for antiquarians, but a living issue. The sons of Greece and the sons of Zion (Zech. ix. 13) confront one another through the generations: on the one side, men such as the Neo-Platonists, Spinoza and Hegel; on the other, men such as Origen, Calvin and Bishop Lightfoot.

Why is this? Well, there is a difficulty about each position, as its opponents have been quick to point out. If Greek thought creates a difficulty for religion, Hebrew religion creates a difficulty for thought.

How can the eternal God be revealed in and through the events of time? How can the relative disclose the Absolute? How can time be the vehicle of eternity? How can any human life, least of all a life ending on a gallows, make the Kingdom of God—the realm of the 'wholly other'—a matter of actual experience? The very expression 'historical revelation' is surely paradoxical to the verge of absurdity. Christ crucified—as the power of God and the wisdom of God! Is it surprising that this was, to the Greeks, foolishness? To quote those famous, almost hackneyed words of Lessing's Inaugural Lecture at Jena in the eighteenth century: 'Particular facts of history cannot establish eternal truths. There is the ugly wide ditch over which I cannot get, oft and earnestly though I spring.'

Christian doctrine makes a three-fold answer to this abiding problem, which is as much an ultimate problem for metaphysics as it is for theology.

In the first place, it fully admits the force of the difficulty, by taking the word 'God' seriously. No real believer can be what Dr Farmer has stigmatized as 'pally with the Deity'. God is infinite, eternal, transcendent, dwelling in light unapproachable, whom no man hath seen or can see. 'Thou art the Lord, and there is none else. From everlasting thou art he.'

> Thou art a sea without a shore,
> A sun without a sphere;
> Thy time is now and evermore,
> Thy place is everywhere.

God is, to use a technical phrase, *totum simul*. That is, in his ageless being there can be no past, present or future. As Professor Dodd has put it, 'in heaven, the eternal world, the Kingdom of God just *is*'. It is 'above the smoke and stir of this dim spot, that men call Earth'. God alone is self-sufficient; as Milton reminds us in another place:

> God doth not need
> Either man's work or his own gifts.

Professor Burkitt once told me a story about E. F. Benson's going to bed as a small child in summer and being unable to sleep. He climbed down out of his bed, crossed the room to the window, peeped through a chink in the Venetian blind, and saw his mother on the lawn playing croquet with some strange people. She was entirely unoccupied with him of course, and it came to his little mind as a shock. He had always assumed as a matter of course that she existed for him and was, as it were, adjectival to him rather than a being who enjoyed a substantive identity of her own. He now learned that she had a life of her own.

Well, God has a life of his own, so to speak, transcending time in his divine simultaneity. Christian thought has ever confessed the ineffable mystery of God's eternal being. Christian worship implies it. Man may only worship that than which nothing greater can be conceived. To worship anything less would be idolatry.

But, in the second place, it is just this which is finite man's difficulty. That alone which he *may* worship is precisely that which he cannot worship. It is high; he cannot attain unto it. Transcendence is really meaningless to him; this necessary category is an empty category.

> O, how can I, whose native sphere
>   Is dark, whose mind is dim,
> Before the Ineffable appear,
> And on my naked spirit bear
>   The uncreated beam?

God, as he is in himself—in the mysterious depths of his infinitude—is utterly inaccessible and unknowable. 'Verily thou art a God that hidest thyself.' Unless the eternal be somehow given to man in history, that is, in the only way which man can understand, God must remain for ever the unknown God. 'God is in heaven; thou art upon the earth'; and, as von Hügel once put it, unless there is some junction between 'simultaneity and successiveness'—that is, between God's eternal life and man's temporal life—man is really without God and without hope in this world.

But, in the third place, all Christian doctrines bear witness to the supreme paradox of the Christian religion, which is this: that God himself has bridged the ugly wide ditch, using human history as his instrument. In the 'here and now' of the time process, God the Omnipresent and the Eternal makes himself known. The Creator is himself Redeemer. Christian doctrine affirms the absolute significance of a particular historical process, and of a particular historic Person who is its climax, its last Word. The concern of religion is, necessarily and obviously, with the absolute, the supra-historical, the eternal. But the eternal God has given himself to man fully, freely and at a tremendous cost, in and through human history. 'The Word was made flesh, and dwelt among us.' It is the most wonderful statement in the Bible.

That the eternal God should give himself to man in terms of time is a great mystery, obviously enough; it is a mystery having no parallel since it is the only one of its class. Nevertheless, Christian faith lives on historical realities and refuses to disown them. Christian doctrine refuses to try to reduce the Gospel to a general philosophic truth. Great philosophical systems, notably those of Spinoza and Hegel (not to mention Hindu monism), have often disparaged history with its hard facts and its unique persons; there is something gross and carnal about its hurly-burly. Hegel can believe in the Logos, a great philosophical idea; but to believe in a Man who died for our sins and to whom we owe everything for our living relationship with God, is to ask too much of the philosopher of the Absolute.[1]

The Gospel is not superior to history in this way. Its secret lies with the divine Saviour who, being found in fashion as a Man, lived the human life 'under Pontius Pilate', and tasted death for every man. The Gospel, so far from being superior to history, *is* history.

What is history? A careful accumulation of all the facts? But that is a sheer impossibility. Facts are infinite in number; there are countless billions of events happening in every moment of historic time. History is always the selection and interpretation of facts. Amos and Jeremiah are interpreters, not of all events that ever were, but of contemporary events, in the light of faith in the God of Israel. They bring a God-given

[1] See H. R. Mackintosh, *Types of Modern Theology*, p. 136.

understanding of God's judging and redeeming activity to bear on a selected series of facts and political events—the life of a nomad sheikh named Abraham, for example; the emigration of Bedouin tribes from Egypt, led by one Moses; the careers of conquerors such as Sennacherib and Cyrus; the ruthless transplanting of a whole population across the desert to Babylon in the sixth century B.C. But in all this the prophets find evidence of the kingly rule of God, his moral judgments, his redeeming mercies, his promises, not only for the issue of Israel's history but also for the ultimate issue of all history.

The events themselves were capable of other explanations, of course, purely natural and secular explanations; but this was the explanation spoken by the prophets. Or, rather, they were confident that it was the explanation spoken by God. They do not say, Thus saith Isaiah, or Thus saith Hosea, but Thus saith the Lord.

Doubtless Sennacherib's private secretary interpreted Semitic history differently. Doubtless the court-chronicler of King Cyrus would have raised his eyebrows at the forty-fifth chapter of Isaiah. Cyrus was a military conqueror and, probably enough, a ruffian of the first order. Just here, however, came a Word from the Beyond, through Isaiah: 'Thus saith the Lord to his anointed, to Cyrus, whose right hand I have holden.... I, the Lord, which call thee by thy name, am the God of Israel. For Jacob my servant's sake, and Israel mine elect....I have surnamed thee, though thou hast not known me.... I girded thee, though thou hast not known me.'

In short, the Christian faith asserts the significance for God of certain facts of history, which gives them their significance for man as revelation. The Kingdom, which is eternally in Heaven, comes to earth through facts which God accepts and transforms. God uses history to make his eternal and holy purposes of redemption actual. A Greek would say that time is only the moving image of eternity. But the Bible knows that it is more than this; it is an actual part of eternity because it has been taken up into eternity by God himself.

But here someone may raise a formidable difficulty. He may say: 'Surely this is arbitrary. Why just the history of Israel and its consummation in the events of the New Testament? Why not the history of, say, the Incas of Peru? Why not all history? Granted that historical facts, human activities, do give actuality in time to the eternal Thought of God, why limit this so narrowly to the "here-and-nowness", the "once-for-allness" of Palestinian history two thousand years ago? Surely the events of which Christian doctrine speaks are only examples, admittedly striking, but still only examples or illustrations of general religious truth.'

This difficulty has been called 'the stumbling-block of particularity',[1] and it is a real stumbling-block. The answer which Christian doctrine makes to it is, in the main, two-fold.

First: there is no such thing as general religious truth; this is an abstraction from historical reality. Living religion is always related to certain events in the past which are peculiarly its own. Real faith never exists *in vacuo*, but in a social context, an historical tradition. Even the most nebulous mysticism which contends that no events or facts are vital for religion, forgets that mystics themselves are not the individualists they think they are; they, too, belong to a continuous tradition of religious experience.

[1] 'Das Aergernis der Einmaligkeit.' Cf. the word ἐφάπαξ in Rom. vi. 10.

The fact is that the present is not merely present; in some sense it comes out of the past and is an extension of that past. That is why Bacon could write: We are the ancients. And, similarly, the only past which matters to us is no mere past; it is our past. That is why Croce can write: Real history is our contemporary.

Thus, those who contend that all events of history are equally significant for religious faith, and that Christianity is therefore as old as creation, forget that natural religion of this kind is a sheer abstraction. This notion of a ready-made natural reason, which the whole movement of history illustrates, is an illusion; it is not natural, in the sense of being independent of the continuous social experience of the community.

Now, Christian doctrine insists that Christian faith is what it is—that it only exists at all—because certain events in the time process have a present, abiding, growing meaning. In and by them a new relationship between God and Man was constituted; it really was. Our presence here to-day in this lecture room is only one of many proofs of it. The Events which constituted what Christianity knows as Incarnation and Atonement created something new, not so much for the historian perhaps (though it certainly did that), but for the believer. He believes that certain facts to which the New Testament bears witness have momentous meaning because they do in fact create a new relationship between God and Man. It is not merely that they exemplify certain perennial truths; they have a creative, revolutionary import for religion. 'No man cometh unto the Father, but by me.' That is what they mean. It is strange; extraordinary; uncompromising. Yes; it is. No satisfactory explanation of it can be given, save that it authenticates itself to the heart of a believing Church, the Church of the Resurrection of Jesus Christ from the dead.

In the second place, the believer adds this: Jesus Christ is unique. No one is a revelation of God in the sense that he is. Perhaps there ought to be another history as enlightening about the will of God as Biblical history is. Perhaps there ought to be other revealers of his redeeming love as remarkable as the Man, Christ Jesus. But in fact there are none. Christian experience and Christian doctrine take their stand, not on what might be but on actuality, on something given. Not on a theory of natural reason (so called) but on *Sachlichkeit*, the factual; what has been and is.

Moral life is only possible for man as he is confronted by eternity. This temporal life of his is confronted by eternity in one unique event in time, of which the whole Bible is the record and the explanation. That event is Jesus Christ, crucified and risen from the dead. In it there is all the majesty of what has happened[1] and can never be turned back into the not-happened, by a reversal of time's wheel. The Cross towers over the wrecks of time; it is for evermore.

> Wisdom will repudiate thee if thou think to enquire
> *why* things are as they are, or whence they came; thy task
> is first to learn *what* is. . . .[2]

To learn what is means facing one fact to which the Bible witnesses throughout and which, if it be true, is amazing. I mean the forgiveness of sin. That is what the Kingdom of God

[1] What Karl Heim calls 'die Majestät der geschehenen Tat', and on which he comments: 'Geschehenes lässt sich nicht mehr ungeschehen machen' (*Jesus der Weltvollender*, pp. 77–8).

[2] Robert Bridges, *The Testament of Beauty*.

must mean if it really is the victorious clue to the history of this sinful world. The most astonishing thing announced by the Christian Gospel, the thing which makes the Gospel, the thing which is 'wholly other' than anything sinful humanity could have deserved or expected—is forgiveness, the redeeming activity of God in history. The prophets witness to this incalculable factor in history, which they can only describe as 'the mighty acts of God'. They testify to a dimension of the otherworldly and the supernatural, impinging upon history and transforming it into the sacred history of God's coming Kingdom. 'Behold, I will do a new thing' saith the Lord. Anything worthy to be called the Kingdom of God must be more than the product of a natural evolution. It must be something about which you can only say, 'This is the Lord's doing, and it is marvellous in our eyes'. This something is the sheer pardon of God. 'This spectacle of the beginning of good, there at the very heart of evil; this establishment of man's kingly freedom through the kingly freedom of God; man in his captive, limited, provisional life...disturbed by God yet borne up by God: is this anything which we can deduce psychologically, or prove or visualize? Is it not rather something outside all history, a sheerly new thing, an absolute datum?'[1] The most amazing fact in the world, if it is really true, is the redeeming pardon of God. The whole of the Christian doctrine of history is built on it. Is it true? If so, why and how?

Yes. It is true. But to see what it means, let us first dismiss what it does not mean. It cannot mean that God is a sentimentalist who makes light of the evil of the world, and that the dreary, desperate battle between good and evil in every genera-

[1] Karl Barth, quoted in H. R. Mackintosh's *Types of Modern Theology*, p. 307.

tion is of no consequence for his Kingdom. It does not mean that the Holy One condones the lies, brutalities and degradations of history. (That would be to make God into a devil.) The prophetic religion of the Old Testament and the New Testament religion of the Cross alike make it clear that God is a God of Judgment. Since he is King, his kingly rule must mean that the pain and woe of history are fundamentally the result of sin, and his judgment upon it. The wrath of God is revealed against all unrighteousness. Because this moral order is of his creation, sinful men collectively suffer as the result of their proud defiance of it. The denunciations of the prophets can mean nothing else. But the prophets never cease to proclaim that this tragic situation which man's selfishness, pride and rebellion bring upon himself is always the occasion of God's grace in redemption. God yearns after Israel. As is his majesty, so is his mercy. Though moral and political slavery be the result of Israel's sin, and is ultimately God's doing, nevertheless God is ever seeking to redeem Israel from slavery. This, too, is the Lord's doing, and it is marvellous in our eyes. God will restore the years that the locust hath eaten; he will remake the broken relationship between himself and his people, and write his law on their hearts for ever.[1] In the Old Testament, as crisis follows crisis, God's denunciations and God's promises are intermingled, simply because it is only in and through the evil situation that God can achieve his purpose of good. No different situation exists upon which God may work. The human tragedy is not only confronted with the divine judgments, as they work themselves out inexorably; it is transformed into an occasion of divine grace. Where sin did abound, grace did much more abound. This is what God's Kingship means; it is a

---

[1] Jer. xxxi. 31–33.

sovereignty of which he alone is capable, the sovereignty of grace.[1]

But the prophets of the Old Testament never said that this new day had dawned, or that the Kingdom had really come on earth. They pointed to it, ahead of them. Crisis, they said, would succeed crisis, until *the* crisis should come, the judgment of this rebellious and fallen world, which would also be the redemption of the world, and the presence of the Kingdom of God with power and great glory.

Now the New Testament asserts on every page that this which was spoken by the prophets had happened. The crisis, the climax to which the prophets had looked forward, was now a terrible and wonderful fact to which believing men looked back, with 'joy unspeakable' (their own words). The Kingdom had come with redeeming power through the dying of one who was completely powerless; the realm of the wholly other had become a matter of actual experience. Whereas the Old Testament is always expecting Christ, the New Testament is always remembering Christ. As the letters B.C. and A.D. indicate after nineteen centuries, he stands at the very centre of history.

At Colmar, there is a picture of the Crucifixion, painted by Matthias Grünewald. It depicts John the Baptist with an unnaturally elongated forefinger, pointing to the Crucified. Christian doctrine might well say that this is the very finger of history, since to the eye of faith all human history, both before and after Christ, points to him.

---

[1] 'Sovereign election means that we are *all* the subjects of double predestination. We are all rejected in that we are condemned; we are the elected in that we are received in Christ' (H. R. Mackintosh, *Types of Modern Theology*, p. 307, interpreting Barth).

The Christian religion means that Jesus Christ is the supreme and central miracle of history. He is the mightiest of God's mighty acts in time, and the earnest of the eternal Kingdom of Heaven. More than a prophet, more than a witness to God's redeeming activity, he is the full and final expression of that activity; he is God's presence and his very Self, under the veil of human life. The prophets had proclaimed the Word of God; he was and is the Word of God. The prophets promised the Kingdom; Jesus Christ was God's very agent and representative in bringing the Kingdom. Indeed, he was the lonely embodiment of its judgment and redemption, as he hung on the Cross and poured out his soul unto death.

Some words of Professor Dodd may be quoted here in exposition of this New Testament conviction that in the death and resurrection of Jesus Christ history reached its supreme crisis. 'The crucifixion of Jesus Christ was an immeasurable disaster, in which the rebellion of men against God came to a head, and sin wrote its own condemnation indelibly on the pages of history. His resurrection made out of the disaster itself a source of altogether new spiritual possibilities for men living in this world. By that two-fold event, the death and resurrection of Christ, the available range of communion between God and Men was enlarged to a point beyond which it is impossible to go. A new era was inaugurated. There was, in fact, a conclusive act of divine judgment and redemption in history. It was the coming of the Kingdom of God.'[1]

To say that God revealed himself in Jesus, or that God was in Christ reconciling the world unto himself, is to say nothing of

[1] *Christian News-Letter*, Supp. No. 31.

real meaning unless we take our stand with the New Testament at one decisive point. That point is where God manifests Jesus as the Son of God with power, by the Resurrection from the dead.

All the evidence of the New Testament goes to show that the burden of the good news or gospel was not 'Follow this Teacher and do your best', but 'Jesus and the Resurrection'. You cannot take that away from Christianity without radically altering its character and destroying its very identity. It is the presupposition, explicit and implicit, of every chapter in the New Testament. At the Cross, the Christian Church sees not merely a striking illustration of the Sublime, but the Sublime in omnipotent action. If the Passion had ended with the Cry of Dereliction in the darkness; if the immemorial problem of evil and pain is only intensified by the Cross; if he came, not to the rescue like a second Adam, but only to the old hopeless fight against sin and death, why should mortals worship this fellow-mortal as their victorious Saviour? If, after all is said, he is one more unfortunate gone to his death, the pathos of man's mortality is increased rather than lessened, and the dark riddle of human existence is darker, for ever. So far from unravelling the knot of human death, this death ties it tight once and for all; and the Christian faith, so far from lightening the burden and the mystery of all this unintelligible world, is its supreme and most pathetic illustration. That the God and Father of our Lord Jesus Christ should pronounce the doom, 'Out, out, brief candle' on him who is the Light which lighteth every man that cometh into the world, could only mean that there is no such God, and that Jesus Christ is his prophet(!). My meaning is that the very idea involves contradictions far less tolerable than the difficulty which it is supposed to meet. Indeed, no man can read the New Testament without realizing that the resurrection of Jesus Christ from the dead, though an inscrutable mystery, is not the contradiction which his annihilation in death would be. His resurrection contradicts all human experience, admittedly. But, as I hope to show in succeeding lectures, Christ himself contradicts all human experience. Unless the whole structure of Christian experience and belief is a gigantic illusion, Jesus Christ is 'eine wunderbare Erscheinung',[1] a unique phenomenon which we can explain only in terms of the miraculous; a particular which is its own universal.[2] Those who argue (with the best intentions, of course) that Jesus Christ is 'like us' are silenced as soon as they are asked 'like which of us?' The truth is that his likeness to us— 'the likeness of sinful flesh'—only accentuates his qualitative and fundamental unlikeness to us, in that his relation to God is unlike anything that our race has seen.

All men, himself excepted, are wanderers in the far country. He alone among men has no need to return to the Father saying 'I have sinned...and am no more worthy to be called thy son', because for him alone the perfect filial relationship has never been broken. He is the eternal Son. He is our elder Brother who leaves the Father's home, coming into the far country to seek and to save that which was lost. He is in the far country, but not of it. Tempted in all points like as we are, he is nevertheless without sin (Hebr. iv. 15). Wordsworth's description of our mother earth as the homely nurse, doing all she can

---

[1] Schleiermacher, *Glaubenslehre*, § 93. 3.
[2] J. K. Mozley's phrase, *Essays Catholic and Critical*, p. 196. Cf. *Limborch*, III. xii. 4: 'The dogma of the union of God and man in one person is naturally inexplicable, being without analogy' (quoted by Franks, *Work of Christ*, ii. 36).

To make her foster-child, her inmate Man
Forget the glories he hath known,
And that imperial palace whence he came,[1]

includes all men except the One who 'though he was divine
by nature, did not clutch his equality with God, but emptied
himself by taking the nature of a servant; born in human guise
and appearing in human form, he humbly stooped in his
obedience even to die, and to die upon the cross'.[2]

If this language corresponds to reality, any sequel to the
Gospel story other than the Resurrection would be incredible
and worse; it would shatter the very presuppositions of the
Gospel story. The Resurrection of the Redeemer is logically
inseparable from his uniqueness; his power in life and his
power over death are necessarily correlative. The language of
the Epistle to the Ephesians (i. 20) means that his cosmic

[1] Ode on the *Intimations of Immortality from Recollections of Early Childhood.*

[2] Phil. ii. 6–8: ὃς ἐν μορφῇ θεοῦ ὑπάρχων οὐχ ἁρπαγμὸν ἡγήσατο
τὸ εἶναι ἴσα θεῷ, ἀλλ' ἑαυτὸν ἐκένωσε, μορφὴν δούλου λαβών, ἐν ὁμοιώ-
ματι ἀνθρώπων γενόμενος· καὶ σχήματι εὑρεθεὶς ὡς ἄνθρωπος ἐτα-
πείνωσεν ἑαυτόν, γενόμενος ὑπήκοος μέχρι θανάτου, θανάτου δὲ σταυροῦ.
The words μορφή, κενόω, ὁμοίωμα, σχῆμα, ταπεινόω, are notoriously
difficult to translate here, because Incarnation transcends our reflective apprehension of it. Here we think in pictorial categories
which St Paul seems to have inherited from the widespread religious speculations of the ancient world about a pre-existent heavenly
Being, a primal Man-from-the-Beginning (Ur-Mensch). These are
preserved in the Hermetic Corpus of writings, the first of which
bears the name of Poimandres. There the heavenly Man is in the
μορφή of God. Being immortal and having authority over all things,
he becomes subject to Destiny and suffers mortality. For, though he
was in tune with the harmony that is above, he became a slave (ἀθά-
νατος ὢν καὶ πάντων τὴν ἐξουσίαν ἔχων τὰ θνητοῦ πάσχει ὑποκείμενος
τῇ εἱμαρμένῃ· ὑπεράνω γὰρ ὢν τῆς ἁρμονίας ἐναρμόνιος γέγονε δοῦλος,
Poimandres xv, Reitzenstein's text). Cf. *The Ascension of Isaiah*, x. 29 f.

victory is the inevitable expression of his Sonship; with the result that to doubt his exaltation after death is to put everything else which the Gospel says about his redeeming power in jeopardy. 'If Christ be not raised, your faith is vain; ye are yet in your sins' (I Cor. xv. 17). St Paul's logic is unanswerable.

The conviction which possessed Christian men from the beginning and which is not only the historic basis of the Church but its animating principle, is that Jesus Christ overcame evil and death and is alive for ever 'at the right hand of God'. In speaking thus, the Church, the very Body of Christ, is not making a vague rhetorical flourish. It is affirming that Christ was really victorious in man's unending battle against Satan and the powers of darkness, and that he could not be held captive by the grave. The Church of Christ owes its very existence to the fact that in this open graveyard of the world there is one gaping tomb, one rent sepulchre. Indeed, for those who begin with the adoring recognition that in the life and death of the Lord Jesus Christ there is shown forth an unbroken communion with the Fountain of Life, in all its fulness, blessedness and glory, anything other than his glorious Resurrection and Exaltation would be the supreme problem demanding solution. From such premises any other conclusion would involve complete pessimism; it would wipe out everything in the Bible save the grim conclusion of Ecclesiastes: 'Vanity of vanities; all is vanity.'

In short, if we are to have a Christian philosophy of history at all, we have to choose between an unambiguously human martyr with whom 'the President of the Immortals had ended his sport',[1] and the Christ who is the Power of God, going down like a celestial Samson into Hades, carrying away the gates,

[1] T. Hardy, *Tess of the D'Urbervilles*, last paragraph.

leading captivity captive, and bringing life and immortality to light.[1] In the words of Karl Heim of Tübingen, 'Faith in Christ involves a question: Is he merely a great personality of the past, or is he the living Lord of history who can tell me with full authority what I have to do, amid all the complicated problems of the present? Jesus the Lord confronts us all with an Either-Or; we must either commit the whole of our life to him or repudiate him passionately and completely.'[2]

Belief in the Resurrection is not an appendage to the Christian faith; it is the Christian faith. The full diet of public worship on any Sunday, anywhere throughout Christendom, is the celebration of the Resurrection of the Redeemer. This is the only sufficient basis and guarantee of Christian faith and worship. It is not tacked on to the Gospel story to make a happy ending, or to hide what, without it, would be the supreme tragedy of history; it is implicit in the story from the beginning. It is from the foundation of the world.

We cannot begin to understand how it happened. The Gospels cannot explain the Resurrection; it is the Resurrection which alone explains the Gospels. Here is the mightiest of the mighty acts of God, foreign to the common experience of man, inscrutable to all his science, astounding to believer and unbeliever alike. But here and only here is an activity of God, wrought out in this world of pain, sin and death, which is the key pattern for the world's true life. Here is the sure promise that life according to this pattern is eternal. This and this alone is the key to the Christian doctrine of history.

[1] J. S. Whale, *The Christian Answer to the Problem of Evil*, pp. 72–3. I am indebted to the Student Movement Press for permission to reproduce the substance of these pages here.

[2] *Jesus der Herr*, frontispiece.

IV

CHRIST CRUCIFIED

THE CHRISTIAN DOCTRINE OF THE ATONEMENT

In that lively and very human book, Mr G. K. Chesterton's autobiography, there is one sentence which sticks in the mind. Chesterton is explaining why he became a Papist, and he puts it with naked simplicity in six words: 'to get rid of my sins.'

If you know any history, and if you know your own heart, you will not dismiss these moving words as morbid eccentricity. A universal note beats through them. It was precisely the same urgent need which drove another man, Luther by name, away from the Papacy. 'Wie kriege ich einen gnädigen Gott?' That is, how can I get rid of my sin, and so get right with him who is of purer eyes than to behold iniquity?

The question is as wide as the world and as old as humanity. It belongs to the ages. That man needs to be reconciled to Something; that there is a tragic disharmony in the human situation which cries to Heaven itself for adjustment—this is a conviction to which the literature of the world bears witness. Oedipus and King Lear are haunted by the same shadow. If you could take this away from Aeschylus, Dante or Goethe, there would be little left but meaningless fragments. Take this away from the Bible, and there is nothing left.

All real religion presupposes the grim and inescapable fact of sin; the language it speaks, in judgment and mercy, is the language of atonement. Communion with God is the very end of man's being, but this is impossible without reconciliation to God. Atonement means, therefore, the creation of the conditions whereby God and man come together. And the heart of the problem or, to use a word which is peculiarly exact, the *crux* of the problem, is this: Who is to create those conditions?

Can Man do so? This is the first big question to be considered. Common sense, not to mention common ethical principles, would suggest that he ought. But can he? The answer of Christian doctrine is clear and unequivocal. He cannot. Christian doctrine takes its stand at the Cross, 'the jagged tree', and from that high vantage-ground looks out on man's unceasing and vain attempt to realize the conditions of reconciliation.

Speaking very generally, man's historic quest for reconciliation with God is always a pilgrimage to the Cross, marked by three stages; stages so related to one another that each is a criticism, explicit or implicit, of the one it leaves behind.

The first is the stage of crude bargaining. Man knows his unworthiness, but seeks to cancel it by bringing his gift and offering his sacrifice. He will thus appease the wrath and win the favour of God. (I hasten to say that here I am not speaking of Old Testament sacrifice.)

The second is the moralistic stage, where it has become clear that the mere routine of sacrifice, as such, is not only liable to abuse; it does not necessarily suffice to reconcile the sinful heart to God. 'Hath the Lord as great delight in burnt offerings and sacrifices, as in obeying the voice of the Lord?' What matters is the inward disposition, rather than the outward ritual act. The way to God is through ethical endeavour;

'to obey is better than sacrifice.' But the pilgrimage is not at an end, even here. The noblest moralism is never the goal of real religion.

A third stage is reached, that of utter self-abasement, when holy and humble men of heart see that even when man comes to God with his obedience and his righteousness, his highest and best, he is still guilty of presumption, still trying to keep an account with God. Mere moralism is a form of pride which befits a man least of all in the Holy Place. It is a further barrier rather than a further means to reconciliation. Only one attitude will do here: 'The sacrifices of God are a broken spirit: a broken and a contrite heart, O God, thou wilt not despise.'

But the pilgrimage is not quite at an end, even there. The progressive spiritualization of man's efforts to earn his salvation has not quite reached the limit of confident despair. The worshipper is not yet saying: 'Nothing in my hand I bring.' As Nietzsche put it with almost brutal insight: 'He who despises himself feels at the same time a certain respect for himself as being a despiser of himself.' The fact is that purely human attempts to create the conditions of Atonement involve an inner contradiction. In attempting to reconcile himself to God through his own activity, however spiritual, man is really putting himself on a transactional level with God, and so denying the very presuppositions of Atonement. Only when the pilgrim makes no sort of claim for himself, even on the basis of his humility, has he reached the threshold of the New Testament where he may fall down at the foot of the Cross.

The Cross is a place where one long road ends and a new road begins; it is a monument to two abiding facts.

The first is that man's age-long effort after reconciliation through sacrifice was no meaningless phantasy. It was a schoolmaster leading him to Christ. That there is no atonement without sacrifice, is a principle running through all great religion; it comes to its climax; it is fulfilled indeed, in the Cross.

But the second fact is that the Cross reveals an old truth in a new, victorious and final way; namely, that atonement must be and is the work of God alone.

'If any man be in Christ, he is a new creature: old things are passed away; behold, all things are become new. And all things are of God, who hath reconciled us to himself by Jesus Christ. ...God was in Christ, reconciling the world unto himself' (II Cor. v. 17–19).

All is of God. This divine initiative in redemption is the characteristic thought not only of Paul the great apostle of Grace, but also of the whole Bible. Grace means love in action; love which takes the initiative, invasively and creatively. 'While we were yet sinners, Christ died for us.'

It should be noticed that this is the dominant conception of the Old Testament, where all Israel's religious institutions, practices and ideas express the redeeming activity of God. For example, Israel's history began with a mighty act of deliverance which Israel owed, not to its own exertions or merits but to the mercy of God alone; the relation between God and his people was not a legal but a covenant relation. 'He hath not dealt with us after our sins; nor rewarded us according to our iniquities.' Indeed it is Israel which first teaches the world that redemption is God's way of being moral. The shocking and wonderful fact is that forgiveness is the divine way of doing right. We are so prone to think of justice and righteousness in terms of law-courts and of the fulfilment of legal demands, that it comes almost as a shock to discover what the Book of Isaiah or the Epistle to the Romans really means by God's righteousness. So far from the righteousness of God standing in logical opposition to his redeeming mercy, it is because he is righteous that he loves and saves. The forensic antithesis with which we are familiar is 'a just God and yet a Saviour'. But the Old Testament says 'a just God and therefore a Saviour'. For the Old Testament as for the New, righteousness does not mean the rightness of moral perfection, the excellence of a man whose moral class is 'alpha plus'. It means being right with God, that is, being put right or acquitted at his throne of grace. Righteousness is God's demand because it is God's gift. All Israel's characteristic religious institutions operate within this context or covenant of grace. The sacrifices themselves were offered to a God already and always in a relation of grace with his people. As a great Old Testament scholar once put it: 'they were not offered in order to attain God's grace, but to retain it.'[1] Indeed, strange and even repulsive though Israel's sacrificial system is to us, its essential meaning and genius was that it was the vehicle of God's revelation to that Semitic people and through them to the world. It was the means of grace, the way provided and used by God himself, whereby he might say to Israel and to the world 'I have redeemed thee; thou art mine.'

It is not so surprising to us, of course, that this same strange, incredible, wonderful fact is the very foundation and rationale of the New Testament. There are many religions which know no divine welcome to the sinner until he has ceased to be

---

[1] A. B. Davidson, *The Theology of the Old Testament*, p. 317 (as quoted in H. W. Robinson's admirable book, *The Religious Ideas of the Old Testament*).

one. They would first make him righteous, and then bid him welcome to God. But God in Christ first welcomes him, and so makes him penitent and redeems him. The one demands newness of life; the other imparts it. The one demands human righteousness as the price of divine atonement; the other makes atonement in order to evoke righteousness. Christianity brings man to God by bringing God to man. The glory of the Gospel is the free pardon of God, offered to all who will receive it in humble faith.

It was this which amazed Saul of Tarsus. What Johannes Weiss called 'this coming of God to meet him', broke him down utterly. Paul discovered that God justifies the ungodly. No wonder that Luther once burst out, in that mixture of Latin and German of which his *Table Talk* is so full: *Remissio peccatorum sol dich fröhlich machen. Hoc est caput doctrinae Christianae, et tamen periculosissima praedicatio* (Forgiveness of sins ought to make thee rejoice; this is the very heart of Christianity, and yet it is a mighty dangerous thing to preach).

Paul discovered, through Jesus Christ and him crucified, that this incredible thing was true. He had 'tried out' the way of legally acquired righteousness to the end, and it had brought him to a dead end of failure and despair. He was a 'wretched man', to use his own words about himself in Rom. vii. And then the miracle happened. Paul discovered that the only really good man is the pardoned man, since he alone has been set free from the selfcentredness which underlies all sin.[1] His life has a new centre of gravity; he is 'in Christ' and no longer in bondage, the result being that he is living on a new level of moral competence. Seventeen centuries later, Kant wrote the

[1] Cf. C. H. Dodd, *The Epistle to the Romans,* a brilliant and lucid exposition of the fundamental theme of Christian doctrine.

famous sentence: 'Nothing in the whole world can possibly be regarded as good without limitation, except a good will.' Well, it is the evangelical experience of the saved soul that the pardoned man is the only man whose will is set free to *be* good and to do good. 'Being justified by faith, we have peace with God through our Lord Jesus Christ.' This does not mean any tampering with ethical realities. Justification means that through Christ's sacrifice on the Cross God calls sinful men into fellowship with himself. The only possibility open to men is the only condition imposed on them; namely, faith in God's redeeming activity. Moreover, such faith is the only soil out of which true goodness will grow.

And lest you should think this a theological extravagance on the part of the greatest of the Apostles, remember that when Jesus Christ speaks of the mystery of the Kingdom of God, the whole conception of merit and reward, so dear to the natural man, sinks into nothingness; I mean that book-keeping conception of religion to which a nation of shopkeepers is all too prone.

Jesus describes the Kingdom of God as a sheer gift of grace. In the parable of the labourers he says that God is like a householder hiring men to work in his vineyard at the beginning of the day and agreeing to pay each of them a daily wage of a Roman penny. 'And he went out about the third hour, and saw others standing idle in the marketplace. And said unto them; Go ye also into the vineyard, and whatsoever is right I will give you. And they went their way. Again he went out about the sixth and ninth hour, and did likewise. And about the eleventh hour he went out, and found others standing idle, and saith unto them, Why stand ye here all the day idle? They say unto him, Because no man hath hired us. He saith unto

them, Go ye also into the vineyard; and whatsoever is right,
that shall ye receive. So when even was come, the lord of the
vineyard saith unto his steward, Call the labourers, and give
them their hire, beginning from the last unto the first. And
when they came that were hired about the eleventh hour, they
received every man a penny. But when the first came, they
supposed that they should have received more; and they likewise received every man a penny. And when they had received
it, they murmured against the goodman of the house, saying,
These last have wrought but one hour, and thou hast made
them equal unto us, which have borne the burden and heat of
the day. But he answered one of them, and said, Friend, I do
thee no wrong: didst not thou agree with me for a penny?
Take that thine is, and go thy way: I will give unto this last,
even as unto thee. Is it not lawful for me to do what I will with
mine own? Is thine eye evil, because I am good?' (Matt. xx.
3–15).

If you would see clearly what this means, look at a parallel
story in the Talmud, which is Judaism's answer to this picture
of God and his Kingdom. It is this same parable, duly edited;
there are the same details, but a different ending. Here, too, a
labourer has worked for only two hours, and yet received a full
day's pay. But to those who complain about unfairness, the
householder answers: 'Ah, but this man has done more in two
hours than you have done during the whole day.'[1]

By what authority does Jesus speak this language of sheer
grace? The New Testament is perfectly clear that his authority
is the authority of God. The mind and act of Jesus are the mind
and act of him who was in Christ reconciling the world unto

[1] Strack-Billerbeck, iv. 492 f., cited by Lietzmann, *Geschichte der
Alten Kirche*, i. 43.

himself. Indeed, as we shall see later in this lecture, unsatisfactory theories of Atonement might have been avoided by the popular mind through the centuries if the theologians of the Church had been more careful to preserve the emphatic witness of the New Testament that the Atonement is, throughout, the work of God. Any transactional theory which would separate Christ from God here, and so rob the Father of his divine initiative in redemption, not only misunderstands the Gospel, but betrays it at its crucial point.

This is not all, however. Man's response is the necessary complement to God's initiative, and any theory of Atonement which omitted it would betray the Gospel in another way. The whole history of sacrifice makes this plain.

What is sacrifice? What was the ancient religious significance of shed blood? And what did the Saviour and the writers of the New Testament mean when they used the ancient language of blood-sacrifice about the Cross? 'It is blood that maketh atonement by reason of the life.' Why does this idea from the Book of Leviticus come to mean something central and supremely precious to Christian faith and doctrine? The problem is vast and detailed, but if we look at Hebrew sacrifice in its broad aspect, as we may legitimately do, two main questions present themselves: What happened at the altar of sacrifice? What did it mean?

First, then, what happened? Something was done; what was it?[1] The sinner is seeking Atonement, reconciliation with God. (*a*) The whole sacrificial action begins, therefore, with his solemn approach to the altar. He does not come alone, but

[1] Here I am closely indebted to the scheme made familiar to us by Dr Hicks, Bishop of Lincoln, in his *Fulness of Sacrifice*.

with his victim. He 'draws near', a technical term for making an offering. (*b*) Next, he lays his hand on the head of the victim, meaning that he is thenceforward solemnly identified with it. What happens to it, in the rest of the action, happens inwardly and spiritually to himself, the sinner. Though it is to take his place in fact, it does not do so in theory; the victim is not substituted for the sinner; the sinner is symbolically one with the victim. (*c*) Next, he himself slays the victim, thus releasing its blood, which is its life. He thus surrenders its life to God, and in so doing he is surrendering his own life. That is the sacramental meaning of the shed blood. In shedding the blood of the victim with which he is now identified, the sinner is symbolically yielding up to God the most precious thing he has, his very life. (*d*) Next, the priest takes the blood, the surrendered life, symbolically into the nearer presence of God, the Altar or even the Holy of Holies. Thus God and the sinner are made one; there is Atonement. But this is not all. (*e*) Next, the body of the slain victim is offered on the altar of burnt offering. It represents the self offering of the restored and reconciled sinner himself, all that he is and has. This offering is accepted by God in the kindling upon it of the holy fire. It is burned. But the burning has a profound ritual meaning. It means the very opposite of mere destruction. The Hebrew word used for this burning is translated 'that which goes up'. As it rises in smoke to the ethereal heaven where God dwells, the offering is transformed. It is no longer gross and carnal and earthly, but spiritualized and heavenly, because God transforms it by thus accepting it. (*f*) Last of all, the flesh of the sacrifice is eaten in a ritual meal. Now that the rebel life has been surrendered and forgiven; now that the carnal man has been transformed into spirit through self offering, not only God and man, but man and man—all who are worshipping there at that altar—become one, in the holy meal.

There, then, is a picture—composite and idealized, admittedly—but nevertheless a picture true in principle to what sacrifice was.

In the second place; what did it mean? Details apart, what was its fundamental import?

Sacrifice is gravely misinterpreted when its meaning is limited to the death of the victim. Thus to isolate one element in the ritual is to misconceive its purpose, which is not the destruction of life but the representative surrender of life. This is the God-given way whereby the sinner identifies himself with the life offered to God. The death of the victim is a ritual means; it is not the end of the rite, or its primary significance. Thus there is no vicarious punishment here, as though the victim were paying the penalty while the sinner goes free. To talk about penal substitution here is to mix up modern jurisprudence with Semitic psychology. Forensic ideas have no place here. The key-word is not the misleading word 'propitiation', nor even the difficult and ambiguous word 'expiation'. There is no thought of propitiating an angry God or of paying him compensation for wrong done to him. God is never the object of the Hebrew verb meaning 'to propitiate' or 'to expiate'. God himself 'expiates' sin by purging or covering it in this his appointed way.

The sacrificial system is a sacrament of forgiveness and deliverance. It is a ritual method ordained and provided by God, whereby sinners may be reconciled to him. God himself has prescribed this veritable means of grace. The Lamb for the burnt offering is his own provision.

If you would see this Hebrew theology in a form of imperishable sublimity, you may look at the fifty-third chapter of Isaiah. Indeed, the Christian must look at it, if only because its immortal words filled the vision of Christ, entered his Gospel, shaped his redeeming course and issued in his Cross. The Servant of God is the suffering Servant. He bears the sin of others. He was wounded for our transgressions. He was bruised for our iniquities. By his stripes we are healed.

Here, indeed, is the doctrine of representative suffering, vicarious suffering. Does this mean 'Substitution'? Yes; though not the simple transference of punishment from the guilty to the innocent. The nations are represented as standing around Israel, God's suffering Servant. They see him bearing the suffering which should have been theirs. And—this is the point—they see what it means: they recognize and acknowledge their sin, and repent. In this sense they share in the sacrificial offering of the Servant, and make it their own. 'It is the complete act,' says Dr Vincent Taylor, 'including the Servant's offering and the onlooker's response, which constitutes the sacrifice presented to God.'[1]

To sum up: sacrifice is two-fold in its meaning. It is the work of God throughout. But, at the same time, it is inevitably the complementary work of man. Sacrifice is both a category of divine revelation and a category of human response. Just as I cannot draw an arc of a circle, without drawing it both convex and concave, so sacrifice cannot be God's revelation without being man's response at the same time. We have seen how disastrous it is if theology ever presumes to separate the redeeming work of Christ from the mind and act of God. To separate Christ from man here, the divine Victim from the

[1] *Jesus and His Sacrifice*, p. 42.

believer who by faith shares in his sacrifice—this too is equally disastrous.

Amid all the multiplicity and rich variety of New Testament teaching, one testimony is presupposed or explicit on every page. Take this away from the New Testament and you have not only radically altered its character; you have destroyed it. The New Testament witnesses throughout to the astounding fact of a crucified yet triumphant Messiah. Its constant theme is the victorious passion of the Son of God.

Look at the earliest 'life' of Jesus, St Mark's Gospel, and you find that almost a third of it is concerned with his death. The earliest piece of continuous narrative in the Gospel tradition is the story of the Passion. The fact in which Christians gloried, and on which they took their stand as they faced and conquered the pagan world, was this scandalous fact of the Cross. 'I delivered unto you first of all that which I also received, how that Christ died for our sins according to the scriptures' (I Cor. xv. 3). It is the characteristic testimony of the first Christian man to whom we have direct access, namely St Paul. The New Testament is saying from beginning to end, 'Behold the Lamb of God, which taketh away the sin of the world.' What the New Testament means by this is an inexhaustible subject, but four things seem fundamental.

First, the New Testament affirms the necessity of the Cross; it regards the Crucifixion, not as a pathetic martyrdom, tragic and unexplained, but as the act of God. Jesus was consciously fulfilling the divine purpose as he poured out his soul unto death. The earliest preaching affirmed that he was 'delivered up by the determinate counsel and foreknowledge of God'. It is not enough to say that he was the victim of human sin, and that Calvary is its supreme unveiling and condemnation (true though that certainly is). Here is divine Action as well as human Passion. Christ steadfastly sets his face to go to the Cross as to the destined and necessary consummation of his mission. 'I have a baptism to be baptized with; and how am I straitened till it be accomplished!' (Luke xii. 50). The shocking paradox, the divine originality of the Gospel, is that God's Kingdom could come in no other way than by the suffering and death of his Representative. 'Jesus', says Rudolf Otto, 'did not believe that he was the Messiah *although* he had to suffer; he believed that he was the Messiah *because* he had to suffer.'[1] It is the mystery of the Kingdom of God that only in this paradoxical and shocking form can Holiness manifest itself redemptively as Grace, in a sinful world.

Thus, Christ not only suffers; he acts. He is Priest as well as Victim. He is the Giver of the Feast and the Feast itself. He is the conscious Master of the situation throughout: 'No man taketh my life from me, but I lay it down of myself' (John x. 18). It is the strong Son of God, not the pain-racked figure of Guido Reni's sentimental pictures, who endures the contradiction of sinners against himself and despises the shame. He reigns from this Tree. His Passion is Action, strong and selfless to the last, when history itself is rent in twain, and he utters the words 'It is finished', and yields up the ghost.

In the second place, the New Testament points to the Cross as a representative sacrifice for the sins of the world.

What does the Cry of Dereliction mean? ('My God, my God, why hast thou forsaken me?' Matt. xxvii. 46.) The history of doctrine is full of attempted explanations of that terrible cry. None is successful. All lose themselves in the ultimate mysteries

[1] Quoted by Vincent Taylor, *Jesus and His Sacrifice*, p. 174.

of time and eternity. It will not have escaped you that the mystery of the Work of Christ is really the insoluble mystery of his Person; it raises tremendous and insoluble problems with which we grapple impotently as we speak of the Trinity.

What we do know is this. It was the love of God—that is, the grace of our Lord Jesus Christ—which identified him with sinners completely and to the uttermost. He who knew no sin was 'made sin' for us. We need this desperately bold New Testament metaphor to express the truth that the Saviour felt the fact and burden of human sin as though it were his own. He bore vicariously the burden of human guilt, and as he utters that Cry of Dereliction we see him stagger under the weight of it. The sinless Son of God was here saying Amen on behalf of humanity to the judgment of God upon sin. And the Church of his Body, participating in his self-offering, has been saying Amen to his Amen ever since. Only he could see and know sin for what it is, because only he could realize to the full the desolation which enmity against God always means.

Is this vicarious punishment? You may set this notion aside, perhaps, preferring to speak of vicarious penitence. Or you may rightly suspect any facile juggling with these well-worn terminological coins. God was in Christ doing whatever was done here. Yet the innocent One himself came so close to sinners here that his sense of *perdition* was real and terrible.[1] It is at this point alone in all human history that sinful men approach nearest to understanding what Sin means to Holy Love. The Man called Christ is the only Man in all history who has seen Sin for what it really is. This second Adam alone

[1] Cf. Calvin, *Inst.* II. xvi. 10: 'He endured in his soul the dreadful torments of a condemned and lost man (diros in anima cruciatus damnati ac perditi hominis pertulerit).'

has seen it with the eyes of God. Wherefore, let me humbly and adoringly confess with all saints and with the great multitude of the redeemed on earth and in heaven, 'he loved me and gave himself for me'; he died, the just for the unjust, that he might bring us to God.

In the third place, the New Testament testifies that here is atoning sacrifice. We 'draw near', and our Lord, our Victim, the Lamb of God, comes with us, for he makes himself one with us in the Incarnation. We crucify him. And he, our High Priest, takes his blood, his very life, through the veil of his broken flesh into the very presence of God. In so doing, he takes our life with him, by the power of the Incarnation and by our membership of his Body. Because we are identified with him, he bears on the heart of his divine humanity all the shame and hurt of our sin. His representative action is atoning action.

> Look, Father, look on his anointed face
> And only look on us as found in him.
> Look not on our misusings of thy grace,
> Our prayer so languid, and our faith so dim.
> For, lo, between our sins and their reward
> We set the Passion of thy Son, our Lord.

Bright's hymn finds a close parallel in one of the Forms of Prayer used by the Church in Geneva in Calvin's day: ... 'Us thou hast honoured with a more excellent covenant on which we may lean, that covenant which thou didst establish in the right hand of Jesus Christ our Saviour, and which thou wast pleased should be written in his blood and sealed with his death. Wherefore, O Lord, renouncing ourselves and abandoning all other hope, we flee to this precious covenant by which our Lord Jesus Christ, offering his own Body to thee in sacrifice, has reconciled us to thee. Look, therefore, O Lord, not on us but on the face of Christ, that by his intercession thy anger may be appeased, and thy face may shine forth upon us for our joy and salvation....'[1]

Lastly, the New Testament witnesses to union with Christ, which comes about and is only made possible through his dying. There is no Atonement without this identification of believers with him. Just as no convex curve is ever without its complementary concave aspect, so all the objective truth about Christ's atoning work is incomplete and meaningless without this subjective appropriation of it. Unless the sinner is 'in Christ', to use St Paul's great phrase, Christ's atoning work has been done for him in vain. It is there, objectively and for ever, but it is ineffectual unless the redeemed man can confess, 'I am crucified with Christ; nevertheless I am alive; and yet not I, but Christ is alive in me. And the life which I now live under physical conditions, I live by the faith of the Son of God who loved me and gave himself for me.'

Our religion does not achieve or sustain this personal character unaided. In the long experience of the Church, this faith-union with the Redeemer is no formal possibility; it becomes a living reality through sacramental communion with him. At the Holy Table the remembered words and deeds of Jesus, as set forth in the pages of the Gospels, become the real presence of the Lord. Believers have fellowship with him, with one another, and with the great unseen company of the redeemed on earth and in heaven, through the communion of the Body and Blood of Christ. This is the end, use and effect of the Sacrament; it sets forth the means of grace and the hope of glory.

[1] Calvin, *Tracts*, ii. 109 (Calvin Translation Society, 1849).

> Behold, the Eternal King and Priest
> Brings forth for me the Bread and Wine.

'Let us understand', says Calvin, 'that this sacrament is a medicine for the poor spiritual sick.... Let us believe in these promises which Jesus Christ, who is infallible truth, has pronounced with his own lips, namely that he is indeed willing to make us partakers of his own Body and Blood, in order that we may possess him entirely, in such a manner that he may live in us, and we in him. And although we see only bread and wine, yet let us not doubt that he accomplishes spiritually in our souls all that he shows us externally by these visible signs; in other words, he is heavenly Bread, to feed and nourish us unto life eternal.'[1]

One question, perplexing to the modern mind, remains to be considered here. As we have already seen, the New Testament undoubtedly uses the ancient language of blood-sacrifice to proclaim the saving work of Christ. This language is baptized into Christ, of course, but it is unintelligible apart from the sacrificial system of the Old Testament. The Church, in its dogmatic theology, its liturgies and hymns, uses the same language.

> The dying thief rejoiced to see
> That fountain in his day;
> And there have I, as vile as he,
> Washed all my sins away.

> Dear dying Lamb, thy precious Blood
> Shall never lose its power,
> Till all the ransomed Church of God
> Be saved to sin no more.

---

[1] *Form and Manner of administering the Sacraments. Tracts*, ii. 121.

Cowper and Doddridge here sing in unison with Bonaventura and Aquinas. The precious blood of Christ is the theme of the *Te Deum* and of the *Methodist Hymn Book*. Roman and Calvinist, Jesuit and Covenanter confess the mystery of the Cross in almost identical language; and Fortunatus sings with the whole Church militant and triumphant,

> Hic immolata est hostia.

But this language about the victim who is sacrificed perplexes and often alienates modern men, not so much because the language of blood-sacrifice is necessarily archaic, and inevitably repulsive to the modern imagination, but because all 'objective' theories of Atonement seem to use it in support of a doctrine of penal substitution which, on the face of it, is immoral and therefore insupportable. It outrages the moral sense. We are much moved when listening to the choir high on Magdalen Tower at dawn on May morning, but we are shocked to discover that the boys have been singing

> Actus in crucem, factus es
> Irato Deo victima.

We turn therefore to Abelard and to the modern theologians who have rediscovered him, content to confess that the Cross is no more and no less than history's supreme demonstration of the depth and splendour of the love of God. Because the 'objective' theories represent Christ's death as necessary, not only to man but to God; and because Western soteriology has used the legal word 'Satisfaction' to affirm the holiness of God's love and the eternal moral realities which are implicit in his forgiveness, modern men protest that such a word makes God out to be a capricious Oriental Sultan, a cruel tyrant who arbitrarily demands the suffering and death of an innocent Victim, that the guilty may be spared his avenging anger.

Plainly enough, this is a caricature of the Christian doctrine of Atonement if the substance of what has been said so far in this lecture is true. Yet the difficulty is real, and it is undoubtedly aggravated by the traditional language of formal and liturgical theology. Two comments ought to be made upon it.

Much popular criticism is irrelevant because it rests on a serious misconception; it is ignorant of those full implications of Christian doctrine which are never absent from the mind of the theologian. Christ's sacrifice is represented throughout the New Testament as a cosmic necessity; he is the Lamb slain from the foundation of the world. How is this to be expressed systematically? There are at least three classic types of answer. Suppose you hold with Duns Scotus, Occam, Luther and Zwingli that the necessity of Christ's sacrifice rests ultimately on an arbitrary divine decree. Or suppose that you hold with Irenaeus and Basil, Anselm and Beza, Piscator and Voetius that Christ died to satisfy the eternal exigencies of divine justice. Or, again, suppose that you follow Athanasius and Gregory, John of Damascus and Augustine, Peter Lombard and Aquinas, Calvin and Twiss, in recognizing that the exigencies of our moral sense suffice to explain why Christ had to die; that only thus could the divine veracity be asserted and the eternal moral foundations of the universe vindicated. The crucial point is that none of these theological standpoints allows you to think of God as a cruel tyrant exacting his due from an innocent Person on our behalf.

In all the classic soteriologies of the Church, he who is

sacrificed is not a human being chosen out from humanity to serve as a scapegoat.[1] That would be the Nestorian heresy. On the contrary it is the offended One himself, the Holy God who is of purer eyes than to behold iniquity, who as the second 'hypostasis' or 'person' of the Trinity assumes a human nature in order to be able to suffer for offending sinners, and in their stead. According to Christian theology, the Being who goes deliberately and freely to his death[2] is not a human personality but the second 'person' of the Trinity, God Incarnate in the clothing of human nature. As we shall see in the next lecture, the dogmatic formula of the Church is: two 'natures' in one 'person'. The link between those two natures is 'hypostatic' and the 'person' constituting the link is divine.

But this is technical Trinitarian theology. Yes, it is. Moreover, however you may criticize it (and in its traditional form it is certainly open to criticism), you cannot escape some such trinitarian formulation if you take the witness of the New Testament seriously. If Jesus is an unambiguously human martyr and no more, the gospels are a monument to a vast illusion, the Gospel is a mistake, and the extinction of the Church is only a question of time. But if Jesus really is the Word of God Incarnate, the problems of soteriology ultimately involve insoluble problems of the Trinity and the Incarnation which no theologian worth his salt has ever minimized or neglected. My point here is that even if you did hold with Duns Scotus that the sacrifice of the Cross was necessary to

[1] Incidentally, our popular metaphors based on the scapegoat of Lev. xvi are strikingly inept: the scapegoat was the goat which was *not* sacrificed, but driven into the wilderness.

[2] 'I have a baptism to be baptized with; and how am I straitened till it be accomplished!' (Luke xii. 50); 'The Son of man must suffer' (Mark ix. 12).

satisfy the divine caprice, you would have to recognize with Duns Scotus (who was not a fool) that it was the divine caprice of Love which sacrifices Itself, and that the Absolute Ruler of this universe (*dominium absolutum, potentia absoluta*) was here being 'cruel' towards himself alone.

Say, if you must, that here Christian doctrine is defective in its scriptural exegesis or its trinitarian metaphysics: in saying this you raise a legitimate and vital matter for discussion, notoriously enough.[1] But do not say that Christian soteriology makes God the Father an Oriental Tyrant, unless you wish to expose yourself to the charge of theological illiteracy. Such a contention is a pathetic caricature of the very truth which the doctrine of the Trinity is meant to conserve. One might as well tell a mathematician that the square root of minus one is mythological nonsense. He would only raise his eyebrows and ask for your mathematical credentials. The most elementary study of the history and meaning of Christian doctrine suffices to show that though no one 'understands' the vast mystery of the triune God, the doctrine of the Trinity is not unintelligible; it is fundamental to Christian soteriology and as such it demands my serious study if I am to evaluate it critically. If a mathematician found me waxing morally indignant over $A^0 = 1$ he would soon discover by cross-examination that I was not only criticizing something which I did not understand, but also caricaturing it. Similarly, the doctrine of the Trinity is easily caricatured; but the truths which it presupposes being inescapable, the doctrine itself is in some form inescapable, and anyone who dismisses it with impatience or contempt will be displaying intellectual sloth rather than intellectual acumen;

[1] See Friedrich Loofs, *What is the Truth about Jesus Christ?*

moreover, ne will thereby be evading the very soteriological problems which his criticisms presuppose.

But another comment has to be made here which is equally important and more urgent. Theological formulations are never sacrosanct; the concept which obscures the essential idea, instead of illustrating or illuminating it, obviously does more harm than good. It is a stumbling-block. Plain men are not necessarily interested in theology. They know that religion is never the preserve of specialists, but the gift of God to way-faring men. If, therefore, certain elements in the technical language of theology only succeed in veiling the light of the knowledge of God's glory on the face of Christ, their use should be abandoned. Unless those who preach the Gospel are pre-pared to expound the special Biblical meaning underlying words such as ἱλάσκεσθαι, ἱλαστήριον or ἱλασμός they do more harm than good by speaking of 'propitiation', or even of 'expiation'.[1] Or, to put the point positively, no man is preaching the Gospel who is not expounding its true, historic meaning and 'getting it across'.

The true meaning of the Christian doctrine of Atonement is that Christ died for our sins 'according to the Scriptures', not according to later forensic or philosophical ideas which use the language of Scripture only to misuse it. Christian theology, as

---

[1] These words all have a common root; they translate Hebrew words used in the Old Testament to describe God's gracious 'annul-ment' of sin. The English translation 'propitiation' is definitely mis-leading: even 'expiation' does not bring out for us the idea of God's grace in 'covering', that is to say 'wiping away', our sin. The vital point is that in the Old Testament God is always the subject, never the object, of the action denoted by these words. So far from needing to be propitiated, he it is who provides the means whereby sin is annulled and forgiven.

Luther insisted, is always *theologia crucis*, because the Cross is the supreme manifestation of the redeeming love of God.

> O Love of God! O sin of Man!
>   In this dread act your strength is tried;
> And victory remains with Love:
>   And He, our Love, is crucified.

V

MYSTERIUM CHRISTI

THE CHRISTIAN DOCTRINE OF THE TRINITY AND THE INCARNATION

You may remember the reference to the Crucifixion in Richard Jefferies' book, *Bevis; the Story of a Boy.* 'The Crucifixion hurt his feelings very much; the cruel nails; the unfeeling spear; he looked at the picture a long time and then turned the page saying, If God had been there, he would not have let them do it.'

If God had been there! That artless comment discloses the whole glory and mystery of the Incarnation. Shakespeare himself could not have made dramatic irony more complete. For the whole of the Christian religion rests on the fact that God *was* there. It is a matter of historic experience that out of this lowest depth to which the race of men could go down, God made his highest revelation. God's mind and act are shown forth out of the very stuff of events which supremely illustrate man's mind and act. This is the Lord's doing and it is marvellous in our eyes.

The testimony requiring interpretation is three-fold. For purposes of analysis we may conveniently consider it as historical, liturgical and dogmatic.

We begin, not with a philosophical dogma, but with the historic fact of Christ in the pages of the Gospels. Who is Jesus Christ, that he should be believed in as no other is believed in by us? Two great answers stand out in the Gospels; we must look at them in turn.

First of all, Jesus Christ was a Man, in the full psychological sense, sharing truly and fully in the conditions of our empirical humanity. The fact which confronts us in the New Testament in all the wonder of its perfection is an actual human life, which was at the same time true human life. He was no phantom, archangel or demi-god, playing a human role on the world's stage, like Apollo in the halls of Admetus, in order to edify and inspire us; 'for verily he took not on him the nature of angels; but...the seed of Abraham' (Hebr. ii. 16).

I think here of Carlyle's protest against the fog of romantic sentiment in which mediaeval history used to be enveloped. He was writing about Richard I and the Crusades, when he burst out, 'Cœur-de-Lion was not a theatrical popinjay with cap and steel greaves on it, but a man living upon victuals'.[1] It is vitally important that we do not in any way jeopardize the truth that Jesus was a Man living upon victuals. The spiteful and ridiculous calumny that he was gluttonous and a wine-bibber (Matt. xi. 19) is precious testimony to the fact that in all things he was like unto his brethren. He not only ate and drank; he knew hunger, thirst and weariness. Consider his bravery, his sense of humour, his severity, his tenderness. To use Pilate's words, 'Behold the Man'—poor, born in an outhouse, working, journeying, praying; tempted as we are tempted. We cannot conceive that Christ in the wilderness was truly pure unless we also conceive that he was able to sin, and that he even desired to sin, but did not. Behold him, healing and teaching the pathetic multitudes, touched with the feeling of men's infirmities, himself a Man of sorrows and acquainted

[1] *Past and Present*, Bk. ii, ch. i.

with grief. He was human enough to weep over the woes of those whom he was not ashamed to call his brethren. Bearing on his heart the burden and shame of their sin, he nevertheless stood in with them and loved them to the end. Utterly clear-sighted, he was the vigorous debater, ruthlessly exposing and fiercely denouncing the shams of much conventional religion. Without a trace of self-pity he went deliberately to Jerusalem to die. His was the highest, holiest Manhood which this world has seen or can see, and at the last—we men and women being what we are—he was nailed to a gallows to die with criminals, the innocent victim of fear, bigotry, jealous hatred, political opportunism and legalized murder. He was crucified, dead and buried.[1]

The essential truth here is that in all things it behoved him to be made like unto his brethren (Hebr. ii. 17, iv. 15). Jesus needed not that any should testify of man, for he knew what was in man (John ii. 25). As Sigrid Undset has put it in a biting sentence, 'to think of Jesus as a frail and kindly visionary with no knowledge of human nature as it really is, or as an amiable young preacher with a special talent for touching the hearts of women's unions'[2] is to be supremely sentimental where he, the great Lover of the race, was as hard as nails. The Incarnate Word is not, in Lord Morley's unhappy phrase, 'the far-off mystic of the Galilean hills'. The Word is nigh unto us (Deut. xxx. 14), as every awakened conscience can testify. The face on which uncounted generations have seen the light of the knowledge of the glory of God, was a face like all men's faces.[3]

---

[1] See the writer's *Facing the Facts*, ch. IV on 'The Fact of Christ'.
[2] *Men, Women and Places*, p. 28.
[3] 'I saw myself a youth, almost a boy, in a low-pitched wooden church.... There stood before me many people, all fair-haired peasant

This brings us to the second distinctive fact about Jesus Christ to which the New Testament witnesses from beginning to end. Here in this human life we meet the living God. It is God himself, personally present and redeemingly active, who comes to meet men in this Man of Nazareth. Jesus is more than a religious genius, such as George Fox, and more than a holy man, such as the lovable Lama in Kipling's *Kim*. He himself knows that he is more. The Jesus, who merely illustrates general religious truths (so called), is neither the Jesus of the Gospels nor the living Lord of the apostles and the martyrs. The Gospel story is a tree rooted in the familiar soil of time and sense; but its roots go down into the Abyss and its branches fill the Heavens; given to us in terms of a country in the Eastern Mediterranean no bigger than Wales, during the Roman Principate of Tiberius Caesar in the first century of our era, its range is universal; it is on the scale of eternity. God's presence and his very Self were made manifest in the words and works of this Man.

This is the second fact which has been indissolubly united

heads. From time to time they began swaying, falling, rising again, like the ripe ears of wheat, when the sun in summer passes over them. All at once a man came up from behind and stood beside me. I did not turn towards him, but I felt that the man was Christ. Emotion, curiosity, awe overmastered me. I made an effort and looked at my neighbour. A face like everyone's; a face like all men's faces. The eyes looked a little upward, quietly and intently; the lips closed, not compressed; the upper lip as it were resting on the other; a small beard parted in two; the hands folded and still; and the clothes on him like everyone's. "What sort of Christ is this?" I thought; "such an ordinary, ordinary man. It cannot be." I turned away; but I had hardly turned my eyes from this ordinary man when I felt again that it was none other than Christ standing beside me. Suddenly my heart sank; and I came to myself. Only then I realised that just such a face is the face of Christ—a face like all men's faces' (Turgenev).

with the first fact from the beginning. They belong together as two ways of experiencing the one historic series of events which believing men know as the Incarnation. The stupendous claim that the Son of Man is the Son of God goes back indubitably to Christ himself; his contemporaries and followers exhaust the available resources of religious terminology to make the same confession. The Christology of the New Testament, in all its developing variety, is no mere *Gemeindetheologie*—the wishful thinking of enthusiasts with little historic sense, a fantastic tune whistled by disillusioned fanatics to keep their courage up. The excessively sceptical rigour of modern 'Form Criticism' hardly commands the critical unanimity of New Testament scholars, but even if it did so it would only reinforce the historic fact that the literary forms known as Gospels are the title-deeds of the faith of Christendom. The Synoptic Gospels are not so much narrative chronicles of the life of Jesus of Nazareth (as such they reveal enormous gaps) as monuments to the selective and tenacious beliefs of the Church from its earliest beginnings. They are the fragmentary signs of a revolutionary spiritual fact—nothing less than the rule of God in power and great glory through Christ, and him crucified. The most cautiously scientific criticism of the Gospels confirms their historical testimony that Jesus' language about himself has at least a four-fold meaning: it implies unique oneness with God, a unique moral authority over men, a unique ministry of salvation towards them, and a unique mastery over the powers of evil. Indeed this Man speaks with the authority of God, consciously and deliberately; and we cannot avoid the questions which the Beatitudes forced upon R. W. Dale, namely: 'Who is this that places persecution for his sake side by side with persecution for righteousness' sake, and declares that whether men suffer for loyalty to him or for loyalty to righteousness they are to receive their reward in the divine Kingdom? Who is it that in that sermon places his own authority side by side with the authority of God, and gives to the Jewish people and to all mankind new laws which require a deeper and more inward righteousness than was required by the ten commandments? Who is it that in that sermon assumes the awful authority of pronouncing final judgment on men (Matt. vii. 21–23)?... These are not words that we ever heard before, or have ever heard since, from teacher or prophet. Who is he? That question cannot be silenced when words like these have once been spoken.'[1]

Moreover the question is answered by the unequivocal testimony, not only of the earliest Christian preaching, but of Christ's own teaching, embedded in the earliest Gospel. The Parable of the Vineyard speaks language which transcends history; it embraces eternity; an uncopyable note beats through the whole of it; if it does not mean that Jesus looked at death and past death, confident that he was therein charged by God with the redemptive recovery of our race, historical evidence is meaningless. 'A certain man planted a vineyard, and set an hedge about it, and digged a place for the winefat, and built a tower, and let it out to husbandmen, and went into a far country. And at the season he sent to the husbandmen a servant, that he might receive from the husbandmen of the fruit of the vineyard. And they caught him, and beat him, and sent him away empty. And again he sent unto them another servant; and at him they cast stones, and wounded him in the head, and sent him away shamefully handled. And again he sent another; and him they killed, and many others; beating

[1] R. W. Dale, *Ephesians*: Sermon on the Trinity (Eph. ii. 18).

some, and killing some. Having yet therefore one son, his well-beloved, he sent him also last unto them, saying, They will reverence my son. But those husbandmen said among themselves, This is the heir; come, let us kill him, and the inheritance shall be ours. And they took him, and killed him, and cast him out of the vineyard. . . . And have ye not read this scripture; The stone which the builders rejected is become the head of the corner: This was the Lord's doing, and it is marvellous in our eyes?' (Mark xii. 1–8, 10–11).

In short, the experience of Christian men confirms the classic experience of the first age of Christendom, that the Man Christ Jesus has the decisive place in man's ageless relationship with God. He is what God means by 'Man'. He is what man means by 'God'. His sinless perfection is a miracle, in the sense that history is ransacked in vain for another fact like it. Wherever men have been met by him, either in the pages of the New Testament or in the long story of his true followers, penitence, the vision of God and a new spiritual life have been one and the same experience. In the presence of this Man, men do not doubt that they are in the presence of something ultimate and eternal. We do not get away from the heart-breaking and life-giving certainty that his judgments and his forgiveness are the judgment and mercy of God. To rebel against this Prince of human life is the very meaning and measure of sin; the grace of our Lord Jesus Christ is the amazing grace of God; to doubt Christ's promises is to doubt God himself and to be without hope in the world. In him the promises of God are either Yea and Amen, or there is no Everlasting Yea, and the long story of human faith and worship is a tragic delusion. Jesus Christ is such that if he be not the destined climax of human faith, he is necessarily the very nadir of human despair.

Two, and only two, critical attitudes are possible towards the documents of the New Testament. (i) A man may refuse to have anything to do with them. He may repudiate them completely, such scepticism being irrefutable. (ii) He may sit down in front of these documents and reckon with their testimony, using all the resources of scholarship to discover what that testimony is. What he may not do, if his investigation is to have any scientific value, is to go behind the documents and rewrite them. That is unquestionably illegitimate. Evacuate the earliest Gospel of the faith which is its living content—namely that Jesus is the Son of God, giving his life as a ransom for many—and no historian with a reputation to lose will look at what is left. To eliminate the Prince of Denmark from *Hamlet* would be no more absurd. Either the Gospels are mythological fiction, or the One who moves through their pages to his appointed end did produce on his friends, contemporaries and later disciples, the unique impression to which men have never ceased to bear witness. The Christian Church knows what is at stake here; it stands or falls with the conviction which originated it, namely that Jesus Christ is nothing less than God's redeeming gift of himself to sinful men. God was in Christ reconciling the world unto himself; it is the unshakable testimony of the Gospels.

I come now to what I have called the liturgical testimony, which springs from the first like a tree from its deep roots. From the earliest days until now Christians have not been looking back to Palestine to revere the memory of a dead Jew. They have been looking up, as it were, to a living Lord, through whom alone they worship God. Not only to the earliest Christians of whom we have any knowledge, but to all

Christians, Christ has always been the object of faith rather than an example of faith. Here is One to believe in whom is to believe in God; to worship God is to worship Christ.[1] Thus the only language about Jesus Christ which has ever been really adequate to Christian experience is the language of amazement and thanksgiving which fills the New Testament, and the great Liturgies; which flows in a steady stream in the mediaeval Sequences and in the Genevan Psalter; which rings like a trumpet in Isaac Watts and in the 'Hymns for the use of the people called Methodists'. The truest dogma is the faith which authenticates itself experimentally in the adoring praise of the Church. 'Out of the abundance of the heart the mouth speaketh.' When Calvin said that to sing the Nicene Creed is preferable to using it as a confessional formula, this is what he meant.[2]

Anyone who has tried to reflect on the mystery of God will understand Hooker's words: 'Our safest eloquence concerning him is in our silence.' A deep instinct has always told the Church that our safest eloquence concerning the mystery of Christ is in our praise. A living Church is a worshipping, singing Church; not a school of people holding all the correct doctrines. Let me add at once that it is far from my intention

[1] Speaking of prayer to Christ, Origen distinguishes between κυριολεξία and κατάχρησις, that is to say, between its literal and its pragmatic sense. His own prayers to the Son, says Bigg, are ejaculatory and brief. Origen knew the danger of Tritheism for those who, through Christ and by his Spirit, may worship One God only. Just because the worship of Christ creates no problem for the heart (II Cor. iv. 4–6), Christian doctrine cannot logically avoid the Binitarian or Trinitarian formulation of its own presuppositions. See Bigg, *Christian Platonists of Alexandria*, pp. 184–8.

[2] 'Vides ergo carmen esse magis cantillando aptum quam formulam confessionis' (*Adv. P. Caroli Calumnias*, Calvin, *Op.* VII. 316).

to seem to disparage correct doctrine here. Doctrine is not only important but inevitable, as I shall argue in a moment. Indeed, an undogmatic Christianity is a contradiction in terms; the Church is now paying dearly for its latter-day contempt for dogma. Nevertheless, believing men live, not by dogma but by the Word of God, whereof dogma is the systematic interpretation.

Open any Christian hymn-book and look with a discerning eye at phrase after phrase in the great hymns; their meaning is inescapable:

> O for a thousand tongues to sing
> My great Redeemer's praise,
> The glories of my God and King...

> At the Name of Jesus,
> Every knee shall bow...

> Jesus is worthy to receive
> Honour and Power divine...

> O Jesus, King most wonderful...

> Head of the Church triumphant,
> We joyfully adore Thee...

> Tu rex gloriae Christus,
> Tu Patris sempiternus es filius...

> Ecce panis Angelorum,
> Factus cibus viatorum...

> Kyrie eleison,
> Christe eleison,
> Kyrie eleison,...

This language means that the Christian Church maintains an attitude of mind and spirit towards its Lord which befits a man's relation to God, and to none else. The most precious hymns of the Church do indubitably treat Christ as an Object of Worship. Here is the beating heart of Christian experience in every age. Moreover, such experience does not necessarily need formal theological expression. For example, Hazlitt's famous essay, *Of persons one would wish to have seen*, is in line with the great central tradition of Christendom. It describes a long and brilliant conversation between poets and critics about the great figures of the past, and ends thus: 'There is only one other Person', said Lamb; '. . . if Shakespeare was to come into the room we should all rise up to meet him. But if that Person were to come into it, we should all fall down and try to kiss the hem of his garment.'[1] Charles Lamb was not a theologian, of course: but he was there putting his finger on the religiously essential thing in the mystery of the Person of Christ.

But we cannot avoid theology, if all this be true. The witness of the Gospels to historic fact, and the witness of all living Christianity to the meaning of its worship, clearly imply a theology. Dogmatic formulations are implicit in this two-fold testimony. They are inevitable, if only because believing men are also thinking men.

Finally, then, there is the testimony of dogma which is given on every page of the New Testament and worked out painfully, explicitly and authoritatively by the Councils of the Church.

Let me insist at once that such dogmatic pronouncements are part of the data of our problem. Only a narrow and peddling historicism will omit them. The Christological debates of nineteen centuries are a monument to the uniqueness of him

[1] Hazlitt, *Literary Remains*, II. 357 (Bulwer and Talfourd, 1836).

whom Christians know as the Incarnate Son of God. The very
existence of a Christology is profoundly significant. There is
no Mohammedology so far as I know. Nor have I ever heard
of a Socratology. It is true that some highfalutin Humanists
toyed with something of the sort in Northern Italy at the close
of the fifteenth century; they invented fancy religions, and a
Litany which contained the petition 'Sancte Socrates, ora pro
nobis'. But that was mere Renaissance puerility, a very damp
squib, and nothing more.

Dogma is inevitable here for two main reasons. The first is
that the New Testament is full of it. It is explicit in the earliest
Gospel, which connects Jesus' superhuman rank with his baptism from heaven. It is explicit in another form in the Gospels
of St Matthew and St Luke, which describe his divine Sonship in terms of his miraculous Birth. The meaning of the
Virgin Birth is ultimately dogmatic: it is one of the many ways
in which the New Testament asserts that the Son of God came
into history; he did not come out of it. In the Epistles of
St Paul and in the fourth Gospel there is a further rich variety
of images and profound doctrinal ideas, all endeavouring to
describe the divine Redeemer adequately and worthily. He is
the Heavenly Man; he is pre-existent ἐν μορφῇ θεοῦ; he is the
Image of the invisible God; he is the eternal Word who was in
the beginning with God; all things were made by him; before
Abraham was, he *is*; he is before all things and by him all
things consist. The Crucified is the Lamb slain from the
foundation of the world.

But dogma is inevitable for a second main reason. Christian
testimony which raises no questions for the heart, does raise
them for thought. They may be insoluble, but not to tackle
them would mean theological suicide: it would be to surrender

the citadel of Christian truth to the enemy without and to the Fifth Columnist within. Carlyle hit the nail precisely on the head when he wrote, 'If Arianism had won, Christianity would have dwindled into a legend'. We are meant to serve God with the mind, even here where the mind is impotent to compass ultimate and ineffable mysteries. The obligation to be intelligent is always a moral obligation. Christian doctrine takes up the problem, therefore, where the New Testament leaves it.

The problem is plain enough. There is an unrelieved tension of opposites in Jesus Christ. The technical formula of the fifth century, 'two natures in one person', is a Greek way of saying that he transcends the power of our logic to make a synthesis of his qualities. The unending attempt to correlate the human and the divine in Jesus Christ is a monument to this mystery.

Of course, an explanation of Christ's person must always be beyond our reach if by 'explain' we mean 'put into a class'. Jesus is inexplicable just because he cannot be put into a class. His uniqueness constitutes the problem to be explained. It is impossible to describe him without becoming entangled in paradoxes. The great merit of the Creeds is that they left the paradox as such.

That is why Melanchthon, Lutheranism's first systematic theologian, wrote the oft-quoted words: 'To know Christ is not to speculate about the mode of his Incarnation, but to know his saving benefits.'[1] Yes; but this sentence was withdrawn from later editions of Melanchthon's work, not because it was deemed untrue (far from it!), but because an articulate and authoritative theology is necessary in every generation, if

[1] 'Hoc est Christum cognoscere, beneficia eius cognoscere, non... eius naturas, modos incarnationis intueri' (*Loci communes* of 1521, Introduction).

Christian faith is to be both continuous with its historic past, and alive in the present.

This does not mean, of course, that there is no danger in such theological speculation. We dare not forget that no part of Christian doctrine is more exposed to the menace of mere intellectualism than Christology. The sordid struggles and barren logomachies which make the history of the Church in the fourth and fifth centuries so shocking, are notorious enough. The more the Greek mind became preoccupied with abstract ideas covered by terms such as *nature, essence* and *hypostasis*, the further it drifted from the New Testament, with its Hebraic interest in concrete religious realities, and its witness to the human *experience* and holy *will* of the Redeemer. Religion largely gave place to speculation; or, rather, Christians of the post-Nicene era could be roughly divided into two groups— those who did not think at all and those who did nothing but think. No one saw the danger more clearly than Gregory of Nyssa, one of the three theologians in Cappadocia who did most to formulate the classic doctrine of the Trinity towards the end of the fourth century. His scathing caricature speaks for itself: 'Constantinople is full of mechanics and slaves, who are all of them profound theologians, preaching in the shops and the streets. If you want a man to change a piece of silver, he informs you wherein the Son differs from the Father; if you ask the price of a loaf, you are told by way of reply that the Son is inferior to the Father; and, if you enquire whether the bath is ready, the answer is that the Son was made out of nothing.'[1]

The grievous danger, both to theology and to religion, is obvious. But the use of anything may not be discontinued

[1] *Oratio de deitate Filii et Spiritus Sancti* (Migne, *Patr. Gr.* xlvi. 557).

because it is liable to abuse; human life itself would come to an end on such terms. Just because we may not disparage dogmatic theology without loss, we do well to heed the New Testament injunction, 'Be ready always to give an answer to every man that asketh you a reason of the hope that is in you with meekness and fear' (I Pet. iii. 15).

So much, then, for the three-fold testimony requiring interpretation. It brings us naturally and inevitably to the classic creeds and confessions of the Church.

Consider, first, the doctrine of the Trinity. How did it come to be formulated, and why? What did it mean?

As soon as the Church addressed itself to systematic doctrine it found itself wrestling with its fundamental axioms. I use the word 'wrestling' deliberately, because those axioms were, on the face of them, mutually incompatible. They were three in number.

The first was monotheism, the deep religious conviction that there is but one God, holy and transcendent, and that to worship anyone or anything else is idolatry. To Israel, and to the New Israel of the Christian Church, idolatry in all its forms was sin at its worst. 'Hear, O Israel: The Lord our God is one Lord' (Deut. vi. 4). 'I am the Lord, and there is none else, there is no God beside me' (Isa. xlv. 5). Monotheism was the living heart of the religion of the Old Testament; it was and is the very marrow of Christian divinity.

The second axiom for the Church's life and thought was the divinity of Christ; and, as we have seen, it carried with it, in some sense, the worship of Christ. The New Testament is not a formal text-book of systematic theology, but there is nothing in the classic creeds of the Church which is not explicit or implicit in its pages.[1] It represents the religious enthusiasm of the early Church rather than the reflective apprehensions of later centuries, and is Hebraic rather than Greek in its attitude to speculation. But even so, its Gospels are permeated with Christology, and it gives us in St Paul a first-rate and systematic thinker whose argument, though complicated, is strong, coherent and carefully articulated, every phrase of it serving to build up a philosophy of history with Jesus Christ as its centre. The soaring intellectual flights of the epistles to the Colossians (i. 12–20), to the Ephesians (i. 3–12, 18–23), and to the Hebrews (i. 2–3), like the great vision of the throne of God and of the Lamb in the Book of Revelation, are assertions of the unbroken witness of historical Christianity to the Incarnation. 'God was in Christ.' 'God hath spoken unto us in his Son.' 'The Word became flesh.' This is the corner-stone of all Christian faith and life, the very substance of the Gospel.

The third axiom was fundamental to Christian experience rather than to Christian thought; namely that God is Spirit, immanent in the whole creation as the Hebrews had known him to be, but now newly experienced and understood as the Holy Spirit of the God and Father of the Lord Jesus Christ. In the days of his flesh Christ had fully revealed the nature of the transcendent God of Israel and his purpose for the world; since the days of his flesh, and notably at Pentecost, this revelation had become a creative, continuous and life-giving experience for all believers.

The Hebraic-Christian knowledge of God is not knowledge of God in his transcendent 'otherness' (which is plainly im-

---

[1] 'Nihil enim continent quam puram et nativam scripturae interpretationem' (Calvin, *Inst.* IV. ix. 8; cf. I. xi. 13, xiii. 3 f; II. ii. 7, xvi. 5; III. iv. 12).

possible to man's finite spirit), but in his active nearness, as it is experienced in nature and history and in the inmost shrine of the individual soul. The most high God, though transcending his creation and abiding in his holy heaven, is nevertheless nigh unto men. He comes upon them 'from a distance', as it were, through his power or Spirit. Just as the wind from the desert Steppes in distant Siberia comes and breaks down the elm branches close to me here in a college court in East Anglia, so God, who is infinitely remote in the ontological sense, is nevertheless experienced as dynamically near, coming upon human life and controlling it, creatively and re-creatively.

For Christians this life-giving energy of God could be described only in terms of the living and exalted Christ, the same Christ who had redeemed men on the Cross in the days of his flesh and who, henceforward and for ever, was the ground and environment of the religious life of the race.

The transcendent God of Israel, who had revealed himself in Christ as the God of infinite grace, was now and always the life-giving Spirit of his Church. In Christ God had entered the limits of earthly sinful experience in order to become the adequate Judge and Redeemer of what One who is of purer eyes than to behold iniquity cannot (as such) experience. Through his Holy Spirit he perpetuates this redeeming and sanctifying activity. The Spirit takes of the things of Christ and shows them unto us.

To sum up: the Bible speaks of one God, and of one God only. It speaks of him in three distinct ways which are normative for Christian thinking. It bequeathes to the Church three axiomatic statements about the being, the purpose and the activity of the living God, leaving the Church to make of them what it can.

Now, fidelity to these axioms being unquestionable, the systematic thought of the Church inevitably involved a further definition of monotheism, an elaboration of the unitary conception of the Godhead, not in terms of Tritheism, but of tri-unity. At first the Church concerned itself mainly with the Christological aspect of Trinitarianism, discussing the problem of the relation of the Father to the Son and virtually leaving the problem of their relation to the Spirit on one side. Not until the middle of the fourth century (Council of Alexandria, A.D. 362) did the Church of the East come to see that what was true of the eternal divinity of the Son must also be true of the Spirit, and that the systematic formulation of Christian doctrine could not stop short of an explicit Trinitarianism. The data of Christian doctrine had been trinitarian from the beginning (Matt. xxviii. 19), but the early theologians virtually limited the field of discussion to the 'binitarian' problem of the divinity of Christ. This discussion tended to take one of two forms.

One form, reflecting Christian anxiety to preserve the unity of God and the divinity of Christ, tended to deny that there is any distinction between God and Christ. This position is known as Modalism, that is to say, Father, Son and Holy Spirit are merely modes or successive phases of the One Absolute God. Just as an actor on the Greek stage might wear three different masks in three different scenes, so there is one God manifesting himself under three passing names or functions. It was quickly pointed out that this meant that the Father was born and died. Hence the nickname of Patripassianism. The implicit tendency of such a doctrine of immanence was in the direction of Pantheism.

The other form, reflecting Christian anxiety not to undermine monotheism, endangered the divinity of Christ. Its emphasis was on the absolute transcendence of God the Father. The Son and the Spirit were subordinate to God; created by God, albeit before all worlds, but nevertheless created. Jesus Christ was a man adopted by God and raised to the rank of divinity rather than the co-eternal Son of God coming down from heaven and taking our nature upon him. This position is known as Subordinationism: its implicit logic was Polytheism. Christ is really a second God, and the Spirit is a third God. Such Subordinationism threatened a reversion to the 'gods many' of paganism, and in the Arian heresy of the fourth century such paganism within the Christian Church became nakedly explicit.

Clearly, the problem was to explain the Son's distinction from the Father, without destroying the unity of God. How are men to think of a divine unity which transcends distinctions without abolishing them? The Church knew what was at stake. It had to fight, as against Modalism, for a real Incarnation and not a piece of play-acting: it had to fight, as against Arianism, for an Incarnation which represents an eternal fact in the heart of God.

The result was the doctrine of the Trinity, slowly worked out and formulated during the fourth century. Christian thought, working with the data of the New Testament and using Greek philosophy as its instrument, constructed the doctrine of Trinity in Unity. It acknowledged in the Godhead, not one Individual nor three Individuals, but a personal unity existing eternally in three eternal modes or functions:

'Neither confounding the Persons, nor dividing the Substance.

'For there is one Person of the Father, another of the Son: and another of the Holy Ghost.

'But the Godhead of the Father, of the Son, and of the Holy Ghost, is all one: the Glory equal, the Majesty co-eternal.'[1]

The terminology of the Greek East and the Latin West differed here, of course, the Latins speaking of three persons in one substance and the Greeks of three subsistences in one essence. Such differences in terminology hardly concern us however, since they do not affect the fundamental meaning of the common formula. Our question is: What did ὑπόστασις (subsistence) mean to Greek, and *persona* (person) to Latin theologians?

Our previous discussion will suggest the answer. This formula, virtually common to East and West, steered between those two tendencies already considered, Modalism and Subordinationism, which became heretical as Sabellianism and

---

[1] *Quicunque Vult*, B.C.P. 4–6. The problem before the three Cappadocians, who gave final expression to this conception of triunity, was the reconciliation of substantial unity with hypostatic distinctions (μία οὐσία with τρεῖς ὑποστάσεις). The divine is indivisible in its divisions (ἀμέριστος ἐν μεμερισμένοις...ἡ θεότης, Greg. Naz. *Or.* xxxi. 14). The Oneness and its Distinctions are ineffable and inconceivable, the conjoinedness of the nature (τὸ τῆς φύσεως συνεχὲς) never being rent asunder by the distinction of the hypostases (τῆς τῶν ὑποστάσεων διαφορᾶς) nor the notes of proper distinction confounded in the community of essence; Basil Caes. *Ep.* xxxviii. 4. This is not Tritheism, as the Arians contended, though Basil (*Ep.* 214) had to admit that the hypostases were counted (εὐσεβῶς ἀριθμεῖν); for One (εἷς) is always presupposed—the unity of the Godhead always belonging to the hypostasis in question (Basil, *de Spir. Sanc.* xviii. 44). We confess one God, not in number but in nature (Basil, *Ep.* viii. 2). Seeberg (*Dogmengeschichte*, ii. 134) describes this not unsympathetically as helpless swithering between the ideas of oneness and threeness: 'ein Rechnen mit Zahlen'. But how is this avoidable, given such a problem? The problem is not a monument to the Greek love of hair-splitting speculation, but to the inescapable testimony of history and the New Testament.

Arianism. The word ὑπόστασις or *persona*, which we translate as 'Person', meant more than 'phase' (thus avoiding the danger of Pantheism), and less than 'individual personality' (thus avoiding the danger of Tritheism).

But does it avoid this latter danger in fact? The question is no idle one since the popular view of the Trinity has often been a veiled Tritheism: as, for example, when the Emperor Constantine died in A.D. 337 and his army demanded three Augusti to succeed him, 'to represent on earth the Trinity in heaven'. Or, to quote Principal S. Cave, 'in the unthinking piety of the Church, the "persons" of the Godhead have been so distinguished that it is possible to read in a revivalist magazine of prayers for a sick child being offered in vain to God the Father and to God the Son, although, when offered to God the Holy Spirit the child immediately was healed'.[1]

That is not even heterodoxy, of course, but sheer paganism, and it has no more relation to the Christian doctrine of the Trinity than has that amusing and probably apocryphal story about Robinson Ellis of Trinity College, Oxford. It is said that some polite sightseers had asked him who were the figures on the roof of his College. 'Oh, the Trinity,' he answered vaguely. 'But', said a lady (with some diffidence), 'there are four of them.' 'Oh, yes,' was the reply, 'Three Persons and One God.'

Our recent question is the crucial one: What is the meaning of 'Person' in the doctrine of the Trinity? The answer is that it does not mean what we mean by 'Personality'. If you convert the Three which compose the Trinity into three subjects, Tritheism is inevitable. The Greek Fathers struggled to guard against this misinterpretation. According to Dr Prestige the

[1] *The Doctrines of the Christian Faith*, p. 268.

patristic doctrine of the Trinity means that God is 'One object in himself, and three objects to himself'. In the one God whom we worship, there are three divine organs of God-consciousness, but one centre of divine self-consciousness. That is, as seen and thought, God is three; as seeing and thinking, he is one.[1]

God is One. The doctrine of the Trinity excludes any activity on the part of the Son or the Spirit which is not equally the work of the Father; nevertheless, as we have seen, the words Father, Son and Spirit stand for distinctive and precious religious realities. With such a paradox, thought obviously approaches a limit where speculation is profitless, if not impossible. Yet it is important to remember that the doctrine of the Trinity is not a piece of speculative scholasticism remote from human experience and need. It proceeds from the facts of revelation and expresses their living meaning for religion. We do not begin with God and end, by some process of rarefied speculation, with the Trinity. We begin with revelation in the fulness of time which is implicitly if not explicitly Trinitarian. God is known to us as Father only in the Son, through the Spirit. Our awareness of God is given to us through worship in the most holy name of Christ; the Holy Spirit of God takes of the things of Christ and shows them unto us. Our life in God is possible only through eternal Spirit, proceeding from the Father and his Son our Saviour, 'which doctrine of the Trinity is the foundation of all our communion with God, and comfortable dependence upon him'.[2]

---

[1] *God in Patristic Thought*, p. 301.

[2] *A Declaration of the Faith and Order owned and practised in the Congregational Churches in England; agreed upon and consented unto by their Elders and Messengers in their meeting at The Savoy, October* 12, 1658, ch. II.

The doctrine of the Trinity, *qua* doctrine, is not the heart of the Gospel. Nor—to cite the almost blasphemous error with which the *Quicunque Vult* opens—is belief in its dogmatic formulation necessary to salvation. But its dogmatic formulation is the ultimate intellectual implicate of the Christian faith, and the historic monument to a mystery with which some of the greatest minds have wrestled. To ignore it as unessential to one's living piety is one thing; to criticize its metaphysical formulation and meaning is another; but to dismiss it with disgust or contempt is only to betray an inability to take theology seriously.

Consider, in the second place and finally, the classic Christian doctrine of the Incarnation. How did it come to be formulated, and why? What did it mean?

We have already noticed that the Church of the fourth century found itself obliged to elaborate and define the meaning of Christian monotheism, in terms of Father, Son and Holy Spirit. This was done at Nicaea in A.D. 325. The Nicene Creed is a short document of one hundred and one Greek words, eighty-four of which are concerned with the Son. That is, the dominant emphasis in this most famous of all Christian Confessions is on the Incarnation. Theology is mainly Christology.

The Son is first described as begotten of the essence of the Father and as being of the same essence as the Father (ὁμοούσιον τῷ Πατρί). Thereupon the Creed continues, 'Who for us men and for our salvation came down, and took flesh (σαρκωθέντα) and became man (ἐνανθρωπήσαντα)'.

The resultant problem is the old and abiding problem of Christology; namely, how to link together the two statements that he is truly God and truly Man.

Here again, given two axiomatic convictions which seemed on the face of them to be mutually exclusive, the Christological thought of the Church tended to take one or other of two forms. There were two main tendencies or schools, associated with the two great cities of the near East, Alexandria and Antioch. The school of Alexandria saw in Christ the second Person of the Trinity incarnate; its thought began in heaven with the eternal Son and then descended to earth. The emphasis of the school of Antioch was different. It tended to begin with the historic fact of Christ's humanity here on earth, and thence to soar up into heaven. These are not necessarily two different Christologies, but types of interpretation having a difference of emphasis. The one interprets Christ as the eternal Word of God incarnate, the other as the God-filled Man.

The defect of each interpretation soon became obvious. Alexandria, emphasizing the unity of Christ's person, really tended to obscure his true humanity. Antioch, by doing justice to Christ's historic life, sometimes came near to confessing a duality in him, as though he were two Sons (δυὰς υἱῶν); the concrete, living unity of his person was threatened.

Thus, the Alexandrians came very near to sacrificing the human Jesus of the Gospel story; in one notorious instance, Cyril of Alexandria explains the limitations of power and knowledge which are recorded in the Gospel about Jesus, by saying 'for the profit of his hearers he pretends not to know in so far as he is man' (σκήπτεται χρησίμως τὸ μὴ εἰδέναι καθ' ὃ ἄνθρωπος, Cyril Alex. *Adv. Anthrop.* xiv). This is Docetism, the heresy that the humanity of Jesus was not real but feigned; a semblance of human life and experience, a piece of pious play-acting.

But, on the other hand, the Antiochenes, ascribing all that the Gospels say about the Saviour's ignorance and weakness to the human Jesus, really jettison the unity of his person. To quote Dr Prestige: 'If we admit for a moment the separate existence of two Sons, the work of Jesus ceases to be the work of God; Nazareth and Calvary possess no deeper sanctity for us than Oxford University and Tower Hill; and God the Son has performed no essentially greater work in Jesus than he did in Moses or Isaiah. Some people think that this is indeed the case. But if they are right, the Christian Gospel is a fraud.'[1]

This vigorous argument is a sword which cuts both ways; in wounding Antioch it wounds Alexandria too; the one is no more prone to lose Christ's divinity than the other to lose his humanity. This is the notorious problem of Christ's Person which theologians in every generation have found to be insoluble. If the men of Ephesus and Chalcedon in the fifth century, like Brentz and Cheminitz in the sixteenth, sometimes look to us like walkers on Striding Edge, Helvellyn, where the slightest false step on either side means a headlong fall, this is not the true and permanent picture of their theological achievement. The official Christology of the Church is not an elaborate balancing feat, as though Cyril and Nestorius, Luther and Calvin, Thomasius and Dorner were tight-rope walkers in a circus. After all, there is a view from Helvellyn, which only those on Striding Edge may see. By confessing One Person in Two Natures, the official Christology of Christendom raises many unsolved problems and lays itself open to damaging criticism through the use of such categories; but it has one great and abiding merit: it leaves the paradox of Christ's Person as such, and in so doing it safeguards the truth as it is in

[1] *Fathers and Heretics*, p. 274.

Jesus, given to us for ever in the pages of the New Testament and in the ongoing life of the Church.

Some criticize this as the bankruptcy of patristic speculation. Is it? All speculation is bankrupt here. If what we know as the Incarnation be true, we cannot escape from a psychological puzzle which is intrinsically insoluble. The *how* of this fact is, as the Greeks put it, ἄφραστος, ἀπερινόητος, ἀπόρρητος.[1] What, then, is the value of formal Christology, and what is it trying to say?

Is it not trying to put into words the vast evangelical truth that in the coming of Jesus Christ into human life, God gave us nothing lower and nothing else than himself? As Professor H. R. Mackintosh has said, sacrifice that touches God's very Being is involved in Christ's being here at all. All the redemptive grace present in the Saviour existed in God, before all worlds; and 'it was out of immeasurable self-bestowal in personal mercy that he came forth whom we know in time as Jesus'.[2] This, in spite of the shortcomings of human language, is what the doctrines of the Trinity and the Incarnation enunciate. Take it away, and you have destroyed the very substance and meaning of the glorious Gospel of the Blessed God.

[1] I.e. inexpressible, inconceivable, ineffable. Cf. Cyril, *Ad Nest.* ii and Basil, *Ep.* xxxviii. 4.

[2] *Types of Modern Theology*, p. 167.

123

VI

LIFE IN THE SPIRIT

THE CHRISTIAN DOCTRINE OF
THE CHURCH

WE sometimes speak of a man's private life, and the phrase stands for a precious truth. If the citadel of his personal being is not respected as something sacred and inviolable; if he is not an end in himself but a mere thoroughfare for others to trample, his manhood is being exploited and denied. You will remember the Roman matron's contemptuous question: 'Is the slave a man?'

But, on the other hand, there is, strictly speaking, no such thing as a man's private life. There is nothing really private, that is, utterly isolated, in a universe where things exist only in relation to all other things; and where, according to the physicists, the most distant star is disturbed every time my son throws his teddy-bear out of his pram.

Indeed, the most private act that any man can perform is to die, to go out of life. As long as he is alive at all he cannot and does not live unto himself. Personality is mutual in its very being. For all its sovereign individuality, the self exists only in a community of selves. The lonely Robinson Crusoe is a possible fiction because he begins as a man before becoming a solitary; but the lonely Tarzan of the Apes is an impossible fiction because he begins as a solitary before becoming a man. Society is only the aggregate of individual selves, admittedly; yet individual selfhood is achieved only in society. In one sense, therefore, the part is prior to the whole: but in another sense the whole is prior to the part. In short, human life demands to be understood in terms of its two complementary aspects, the individual and the corporate, the part and the whole. Each has to be interpreted in terms of the other.

But here we meet a difficulty: let me try to state it on behalf of an objector. Someone may say: 'Surely religion is a man's private affair. Has not a great Cambridge mathematician defined religion as what a man does with his solitariness? After all, what could be more private than the evangelical experience of the saved soul, experience which has found classic expression in words such as these:

> His dying crimson like a robe,
>   Spreads o'er his body on the tree:
> Then am I dead to all the globe,
>   And all the globe is dead to me.

Surely that personal note is the only authentic note of true religion. The burdened and needy sinner cannot come to God by proxy; no one may take his place in the secret place. The greatest hymn in the English language does not begin

> When *we* survey the wondrous Cross.

It is I who must come to the Mercy-Seat, I myself alone, if I am to appropriate the saving benefits of the Crucified. And though Edward Gibbon once described the word "I" as the most indecent of the personal pronouns, can you deny that its absence would be indecent here at the Cross? That great hymn ends, very properly, on the same personal note with which it begins:

> Love so amazing, so divine,
>   Demands my soul, my life, my all.'

Now, to all this, Christian doctrine certainly says Amen without any hesitation. It not only admits, it insists that religion is always inescapably personal. Religion without this would be like love without any lovers to illustrate it. But this truth does not stand alone; this is not the whole truth about even the most sacredly intimate religious experience.

Let us notice again what the issue is. It is contended that we meet God individually and we meet him alone, and this is certainly true. 'Except a man be born again, he cannot see the kingdom of God.' This, again, is no idle metaphor. The travail of rebirth differs from the travail of birth in that it takes place in one's own heart, and its pangs are all one's own. Not even your own mother can bear this for you. But here too the whole is conceptually and essentially prior to its parts; the Holy Catholic Church is both logically and chronologically prior to its individual members with their individual experiences. Christian doctrine knows nothing of an atomistic individualism. Though an intensely personal matter, faith is never a purely private matter. Man, as God has made him, is an individual ego, but not an isolated ego. A self-centred isolation is the corruption of human nature; it is the result and very illustration of sin. As I tried to show in my first two lectures, man is man only by virtue of his relation to God, a relation which carries with it and determines his relation to his fellow men. Just as we cannot really escape from God into rebellious isolation from him, so our isolation from one another, due to our sin, is an illusion. Human relationships do not cease to be because man is self-centred; they persist as a ghastly caricature of what they were meant to be. They go bad; they turn sour. This world becomes a jungle instead of being the Father's house and our home. Man's proud egocentricity punishes him not by destroying his relation to God and man (which is impossible), but by turning it inside out and so making what might have been a blessing into a curse.

This being so, redemption must mean the restoration of that community of sons which God wills eternally. Christ's work of reconciliation re-establishes not only our filial relation to God, but also our fraternal relation to one another. These are not two different facts requiring co-ordination: they are correlative: indeed they are one and the same fact. Christ is the head of a new humanity. To be saved by him is to be incorporated into the new community, his Church, of which he is not so much Founder as Foundation. The thought of the New Testament about redemption is as much corporate and communal, as it is individual and personal. This two-fold truth is the key to the Christian doctrine of the Church.

Tennyson was not wrong, of course, in saying that the main miracle of this universe is that 'Thou art Thou'; that 'I am I'. Man's personality is the wonder of God's creation. But the corruption of the best is the worst. The essential sin is pride, that is, where man's personality is rotten at its very core. And this sin is not less but more deadly when it takes the form of spiritual pride. Christ's denunciation of the Pharisees surely means that the wrong kind of religious individualism is the deadliest sin of all, just because Satan there disguises himself as an angel of light. It is not only the 'main miracle' but also the main tragedy of the universe, that 'I am I'. I need redemption from myself into the glorious liberty of the children of God. Only in that new and God-given context can I really find myself. You probably know Myers' poem *St Paul*, which tells you rather more about Frederick Myers than it does about St Paul. It mirrors its writer rather than his subject.

What is this lengthy introspection but self-centredness at its most subtle and most dangerous? It is hardly surprising that one comment on it has taken the form of parody:

> I, who am I, and no man may deny it;
> I, who am I, and none shall say me nay;
> Lo, from the housetops to the hills, I cry it—
> I have forgotten what I meant to say.

Certain it is that for St Paul, and for New Testament Christianity, to be a Christian is to be a member of a living organism whose life derives from Christ. There is no other way of being a Christian. In this sense, Christian experience is always ecclesiastical experience. The Gospel of pardon reaches you and me through the mediation of the Christian society, the living body of believers in whose midst the redeeming Gospel of Christ goes out across the centuries and the continents. To say that Christ founded the Church and to say that he mediates to needy men the assurance of forgiveness, is to say one and the same thing. The Work of Christ is perpetuated only in the Church of Christ. To adopt an emendation of the children's hymn:

> Jesus loves me, this I know,
> For my mother tells me so.

If the doctrine of Apostolic Succession means anything which excludes this, it is out of line with the only historic realities which matter. For the Apostolic conception of the Church is indubitably a brotherhood of those who are 'in Christ', loving spirits who set others on fire. It is the growing Society of the Kingdom of God. The Kingdom of God is present in Jesus Christ, through whom God gives the Kingdom by the agency of his Holy Spirit to those who will receive it.

The New Testament describes the life of this society as life in the Spirit. The Hebrew word for 'spirit' originally denoted 'wind', that mighty energy of the desert from which Israel sprang. The Church, as the community of the Redeemed, is the new Israel of God. It is a Body whose Head is Christ and whose members are individual believers. Looking back to Pentecost, its birthday, it uses this desert metaphor to describe the spiritual energy animating it. The Word and the Sacraments are the organs of its supernatural life, the means of grace. The Holy Spirit, proceeding from the Father and the Son is ever the supreme agent of grace.

In short, the Christian life is not accidentally but necessarily corporate, always and everywhere. It is so by its very nature as the Body of Christ. The Holy Catholic Church, whether Greek, Roman or Reformed, has never thought of Churchmanship as an 'extra' to personal faith, an 'optional subject' so to speak, for those who happen to be gregariously inclined. A true and saving knowledge of the Redeemer is impossible without it. It is sometimes suggested that Christian doctrine speaks with this emphasis because mere individualism is now discredited in every field of thought and action; because of Coleridge with his philosophy of the corporate, or because Sir Walter Scott taught the nineteenth century the profound meaning of historical tradition. In fact, of course, vital Christianity has never existed apart from that Body of Christ, through which the Spirit takes of the things of Christ and shows them to every generation. The Oxford Movement was not an innovation but a recovery. The magnificent High Churchmanship of Calvin was nothing peculiar; it is in line with the Churchmanship of Innocent III and Gregory VII; Calvin is the Cyprian of the sixteenth century; his massive theological system and his momentous historical importance find their explanation in the four words which sum up the whole of Christian history, Ubi Christus ibi Ecclesia.

At once we meet a difficulty which needs no labouring. From the viewpoint of ecclesiastical polity the Church is divided. Christians do not face the world with any authoritative unanimity as to what the Church believes about itself. So far from being Christ's seamless robe, the visible Church is a coat of many colours.

Thus a public lecturer on the Christian doctrine of the Church is in an awkward position. He has to choose between two courses: either he will belittle the difficulties and run away from them, his lecture degenerating into a graceful but heartfelt appeal for ambiguity; or he will recognize and state the historic difficulties, the different presuppositions and interpretations which here divide sincere and devoted Christians from one another. If there are any positive principles, only in this way may he hope to get at them. Moreover, he will gain nothing by attempting to conceal his own point of view; you would not thank me if, out of a mistaken sense of courtesy, I watered down the historically conditioned ecclesiastical polity which I know and understand, into something vague enough to suit all tastes. It would suit none of course. To pretend that different doctrines of the Church are only aspects of one and the same doctrine would be frivolous, and palpably false to historical and theological fact. Mere syncretism will get us nowhere. Chesterton once defined syncretism in a grotesque but exact epigram as 'religion going to pot'; and I need not pause to win your assent to what is a matter of common experience, namely, that religion is solid meat and not the contents of the stock-pot boiled down into a smooth mush of vague religiosity. Every truly religious man, be he Hindu or Mohammedan, Jew or Christian, Jesuit or Puritan, is a man of precise notions; like the sons of Eli he prefers raw flesh to sodden.

Sidney Smith once witnessed a noisy slanging-match between two women who were standing at their doors and facing one another across a mean street. As he turned away he said to his friend: 'These women will never agree because they argue from different premis(s)es.' And yet, of course, that is all that anybody can do. I have to begin from where I live. I happen to be a minister of the Churches of the Congregational Order, one who stands gratefully and proudly in the Reformed tradition of Genevan High Churchmanship. It is from those premis(s)es that I have to look respectfully and sympathetically at great differences of emphasis in ecclesiology.

The study of Church History is not unlike a visit to Madame Tussaud's, where you find yourself in front of the distorting mirrors. There are two in particular which hold your attention. The one makes you look like a clothes-prop; the other makes you look like a barrel. You recognize yourself in both mirrors; it is *your* overcoat and muffler, your walking-stick and your face; but the exaggerations are deplorable, almost painful. It is a relief to turn to a plane mirror where, in spite of obvious and admitted imperfections, you see the normal thing. You wish it were better, but are glad it is no worse.

My meaning is that Church History is a series of mirrors in which Christianity sees itself, now with this and now with that element exaggerated and even distorted, in relation to the whole. The elements are the same in every case, remember. In each mirror you cannot fail to see the Bible; the Institutional

Church as a local fact—a gathered company of believers; a Ministry duly ordained; the observance, every Lord's Day, of the Feast of the Saviour's Resurrection from the dead; the preaching of the Word; the administration of the Sacraments; ecclesiastical discipline; Christian character and even sainthood; the most unchristian hypocrisies and sins. No Church has a monopoly in any of these facts; you cannot put a denominational ring-fence around them. Whether you look to Canterbury or Constantinople, to Dayton (Tennessee) or to Cornish Methodism, to Wittenberg or Upsala, to Rome or Geneva—you see the same marks of the Holy Catholic Church on earth, the same lineaments of him who is the Head of the whole Body. The differences are real, even enormous; but the essential and constitutive facts are the same. There are important differences of metre and accent, but all within the same sequence of musical notes.

Look first into this mirror on the right. Here the Church is visible as a great and impressive Institution. It is a fellowship of believers too, of course, who hold the true faith and participate in the Sacraments. But its specific *differentia* lies in centralized organization which is here at the maximum. This Church resembles a State and, what is more, an Autocracy. No system of ecclesiastical absolutism could be more thoroughgoing than one which reaches its logical climax in the divinely guaranteed infallibility of its head. This Church conceives of its nature and function in terms of a legalism which is defined with an almost brutal clarity. Its doctrine is as clear as it is uncompromising. Because it is the actual and only depository of salvation, outside it there is no salvation. Loyalty to Christ is defined as obedience to his Vicar on earth. Instead of thinking of the Church in terms of God, this system thinks of

God in terms of the Church. Through its divinely given system of mediation alone may the sinner find God. Its very *esse* lies in its ruling hierarchy rather than in the personal faith of its members. To quote the celebrated definition of Bellarmine (*De ecclesia militante*, c. 2): 'Our doctrine of the Church is distinguished from the others in this, that while all others require inward qualities (internas virtutes) in everyone who is to be admitted to the Church, we believe that all the virtues, faith, hope, charity and the others, are found in the Church. We do not think that any inward disposition (ullam internam virtutem) is requisite from anyone in order that he may be said to be part of the true Church whereof the Scriptures speak: all that is necessary is an outward confession of faith and participation in the sacraments (sed tantum externam professionem fidei et sacramentorum communionem). The Church, in fact, is a company of men (coetus hominum) as visible and palpable as the assembly of the Roman people, or the Kingdom of France, or the Republic of Venice.'

I cite this to illustrate a doctrine which explicitly excludes from the idea of the Church all subjective and personal elements. An Encyclical of Pope Pius X goes further and is more explicit: 'The Church is the mystical Body of Christ, a Body ruled by Pastors and Teachers, a society of men headed by rulers having full and perfect powers of governing, instructing and judging. It follows that this Church is essentially an unequal society, that is to say, a society comprising two categories of persons; pastors and the flock; those who hold rank in the different degrees of the hierarchy and the multitude of the faithful. And these categories are so distinct in themselves that in the pastoral body alone reside the necessary right and authority to guide and direct all the members towards the goal of the society. As for the multitude, it has no other right than that of allowing itself to be led and, as a docile flock, to follow its shepherds.'[1]

Here, plainly enough, there is no room for a purely pragmatic or utilitarian theory of episcopacy which would argue that the office of the bishop is of the *bene esse* of the Church, and an historic means whereby God has greatly blessed his people. The bishop is rather the very *esse* of the Church; his hands are the indispensable link between the blessed Trinity and the ordinary man; salvation is therefore impossible apart from the priestly hierarchy. My only comment is that this doctrine of an exclusively mediatorial priesthood is indubitably alien both to the letter and the spirit of the New Testament. Salvation through bishops, through presbyters, or through 'the priesthood of all believers' is a distortion of the faith once for all delivered to the saints. It is a return to that legalism after which we fallen men are always hankering, whether we call ourselves Catholics or Protestants, whether we say 'I am of Rome' or 'I am of Geneva'. Just because the Church's one sufficient treasure is the Gospel of God's sheer grace in all its sovereign sufficiency, we sinners are uneasy. We want to earn this treasure. We ask to be entangled again in the yoke of bondage. We manufacture legal guarantees. 'The essence of it is that an institution with official rule seems a better security than a fellowship with Divine gifts.... Against this veiling of the truth in flesh', says John Oman, 'it is in vain to be angry. Till man is wholly spiritual it will be God's necessary way with him.'[2]

But now, in the second place, will you look into this mirror on the left? Here, too, is distortion, but of an exactly opposite

[1] *Vehementer*, 11 February, 1906.
[2] Art. 'Church', *E.R.E.* iii. 622a, 623b.

kind. Here the aspect of the Church is individualist rather than totalitarian; it is not a great corporate Institution taking precedence of the individual, but the reverse. The believing individual being the important fact, the outward forms and corporate institutions of the visible Church tend to be of secondary importance. The Church is essentially a fellowship of individuals who have faith in Christ and seek to walk together in obedience to him. Right and impressive though this conception is, if it excludes certain other conceptions it is a distortion of the whole truth about the Church. Indeed it might be regarded as the antithesis of the Roman thesis.

I am reminded here of a profound remark which Pym made in the House of Commons when this very issue was being fought out in the sphere of politics: 'If the Prerogative overcome Liberty it will grow to Tyranny; if Liberty overcome the Prerogative it will grow to Anarchy.' *Mutatis mutandis* these wise words apply as much to ecclesiastical polity as to political science.

The weakness of mere association in the name of spiritual freedom is that it degenerates all too easily into something local and sectarian. After all, Church history is eloquent of the weakness as well as the strength of movements such as Montanism, Donatism and Anabaptism. The strength of all such reforming and enthusiastic movements lies in the truth that the Church does not make the believing individuals what they are: they are ceaselessly making it what it is. The part does come before the whole in the sense that without the parts there would be no whole. The weakness of such movements, however, lies in their blindness to the history which they cannot escape. For in a truly spiritual sense it is the Church which makes the individual what he is, because it is the Church alone which mediates Christ to him. In short, the peril of an excessive subjectivism is three-fold.

First, there is the peril of an Independence which loses sight of oecumenical realities. The Holy Catholic Church is absorbed into the local, gathered churches. About this one can only say that though the gathering together of a local congregation of believers for the breaking of bread and prayers is the oldest ecclesiastical fact in Christendom, it has never been the whole truth about the Church. The theory that each particular congregation is conceptually and constitutionally prior to the great body of the Church Catholic, is unknown not only to the Church of the New Testament, but also to classic Protestantism.[1]

Secondly, there is the peril of an Individualism which makes its appeal to the inwardness of the Word and finds the sanctuary within the individual heart. Hans Denck and Sebastian Franck, David Joris and George Fox illustrate its essential nobility, but its dangers are writ large in history. A healthy dread of formalism in religion has often worked out as an unhealthy indifference to all outward forms, and blindness to the truth that the life of the Church through its worship, ministry and sacraments is not a help to religion,—it is religion.

Thirdly, there is the peril of a Perfectionism which so easily becomes the sin of spiritual pride, and ends as the sin of schism. Just because 'Reformation without tarrying for any' is sometimes the call of God himself, the Devil's work has often been done in its name. And here no branch of the whole Church can escape condemnation, Greek, Roman, Lutheran, Reformed, Anglican, Puritan, Methodist. I think here of Calvin's striking words in defence of the ordinary people of

[1] See *Additional Note* at the end of this lecture, on the Reformation and Churchmanship.

a parish or city or nation, who make no high claim to be 'righteous overmuch'. Speaking of the Perfectionists or Rigorists, 'esprits phrenetiques' as he calls them, he says: 'Let them remember that the Word of God and his holy Sacraments have more virtue in conserving the Church than the vices of some of its members have in dissipating it.'[1] 'We have no right', he says in another place, 'lightly to abandon a Church because it is not perfect.'[2] The spectacle of a divided Christendom provoked these words: the history of a divided Protestantism confirms their wisdom.

To sum up: the Church cannot see the truth about its nature in either of these distorting mirrors, the one on the right hand, the other on the left. Neither thesis nor antithesis is free from distortion and error. Moreover, the true synthesis does not exist. There is no perfect mirror hanging between the other two, 'not having spot, or wrinkle, or any such thing'. All branches of the Church are subject to grievous mixture and error. None is pure. The pure Church, Christ's very Bride, is in heaven. The life we live is life on earth, historically conditioned. Its tensions and troubles belong to the mystery of sin in which all earthly existence is involved. Escape out of it we cannot. But freedom within it and sufficient light upon it we may have, in Christ, through faith. In him existence

[1] *Inst.* IV. i. 16.

[2] *Inst.* IV. i. 12; ii. 5. Calvin had a *magnus et intimus horror* of *aliquod in ecclesia schisma* (*Opera*, xb. 351). To Cranmer's letter to him (1552) suggesting a meeting of learned and godly men, in view of the urgent necessity of doctrinal agreement among Protestants, especially about the Sacrament, Calvin replies that he would willingly cross ten seas, if necessary, to achieve such an end ('ne decem quidem maria, si opus sit, ob eam rem traicere pigeat'). The letters are given in Cranmer, *Remains and Letters*, p. 432 (Parker Society).

becomes life. Yet it is life here and now in the body with all that this means; a progress in holiness, but not perfection. So it is with the Church. This brings us, therefore, to the concrete problem: What are the marks of a true Church?

The first mark of the Church is that it belongs to Christ, its one invisible Head. The Bride belongs to the Bridegroom alone. In theory, of course, all Christians recognize this, the Greeks and the Protestants explicitly; and even the Romans, implicitly, in spite of their claim that the Bishop of Rome was and is appointed by Christ to be his Vicar on earth, the visible head and absolute ruler of his Church. All Christians know that the Rights of the Redeemer are Crown Rights, however prone they may be to act as though either an Italian Bishop or an English King or a Puritan Parliament or an individual conscience were Head of the Church.

The Church is one in spite of its divisions; just as Humanity is one, in spite of its national and racial divisions. It is because there is no Congregational Church, no Latin or Greek, no Presbyterian or Methodist Church but one Church which is the very creation of the Incarnate Word, that Roman as well as Protestant, Puritan as well as Monk, Jesuit as well as Covenanter, are all Catholics, confessing one Lord, one Faith, one Baptism, one God and Father of all, who is above all and through all and in all. All Christians bless the same sacred Name by which they have been called; all partake of the same holy food (even those to whom the Cup is denied); all have been buried with Christ in Baptism and raised with him unto life eternal. All adore the mystery of the redeeming grace of God in its absolute sovereignty. The great New Testament doctrines of Election and Justification by Faith are thus the sheet-anchor of all true Churchmanship. They proclaim that our salvation is the sovereign act of the living God, untouchable by human activity or weakness, unshakable in its finality. Our citizenship is in heaven. The Church is, in one inescapable sense, the invisible church; the great company of the elect of God, stretching beyond the sight and the measurement of any man or any God-given institution. God is not bound even by institutions of his own appointing. He alone knows those who are his. In the words of St Augustine, 'there are many sheep without, and many wolves within'.[1] When Savonarola was about to be burnt at the stake in fifteenth-century Florence, the Bishop of Vasona, in his embarrassment, bungled the usual formula, saying: 'I separate thee from the Church militant and triumphant.' At once the martyr interjected: 'From the Church militant, not triumphant; for this is not thine' (hoc enim tuum non est). The Bishop accepted the correction, saying: 'Amen. May God number you therein.' Even Canon Law does not presume to legislate for God. It legislates on behalf of God, who alone knows whether its legislation is ratified in heaven. The same great truth of the absolute sovereignty of God gives point to the well-known words: 'Deus non alligatus sacramentis suis: nos autem alligamur.' And Calvin, whose doctrine of the Church and the Sacraments was no less rich and profound than that of mediaeval theology, made the same point when he wrote: 'The thief on the Cross became the brother of believers, though he never partook of the Lord's Supper.'

The first mark of the Church, then, is that it is more and other than an earthly society, a mere product of history. It is

[1] 'Secundum occultam Dei praedestinationem plurimae sunt foris oves, plurimi lupi intus' (Aug. *Homil. in Johan.* xlv).

invisible, that is, a spiritual fact, originating and depending wholly upon the sovereign grace of God, which no power on earth can either give, condition or take away. It is the whole company of the elect that have been, are or shall be, on earth and in heaven: one Body, whose sole Head is Christ.

But we cannot stop here. To do so would be to leave everything in the air, and to refuse to 'come down to brass tacks'. It would be an Irish result if the only discernible mark of the Church were its invisibility. How is the Church recognized and known in this world of time and sense? Who are its members? To say that God alone knows would be to make the Church irrelevant.

Thus, it is the second mark of the Church that, empirically considered, it is necessarily visible and institutional. This wonderful and sacred mystery is mediated to us through the visible and empirical; sacred Scriptures; sacred rites and sacraments, the outward, visible and efficacious signs of inward and spiritual realities; sacred offices of Christian ministry; sacred seasons, buildings, forms. Life in the spirit is never disembodied; it is incarnate in a Body whose organs are Word, Sacraments and Ministry. Indeed, the visible Church is the divinely given medium whereby God's sovereign grace is shed abroad. It is the 'means of grace', from which all others draw their life. It is the supreme agency of mediation following upon that of the Incarnate Son of God himself. That is why the Visible Church is rightly known by all Christians as 'an extension of the Incarnation'. For all Christians the Church is at once a fellowship and an institution, two correlative facts, each of which may only be defined in terms of the other. Christian life, as we have seen all along, is lived in terms of a tension between the individual and the ecclesiastical; between the local and the oecumenical; between the spontaneity of that Holy Spirit which is as lightning when it goeth from the East unto the West, and the settled tradition of Christian thought and praxis whereby all things are done decently and in order.

Thus, God's 'new creation by water and the Word' is seen and known wherever the Word is faithfully preached and heard, the Gospel Sacraments are purely administered and godly discipline is a reality. These are earthen vessels, but they hold treasure, nothing less than the unsearchable riches of Christ. To quote Luther: 'If thou wilt be saved thou must begin with the faith of the Sacraments (A fide sacramentorum tibi incipiendum est, si salvus fieri voles).'[1] And, as he says in another typical sentence, 'There would be no Bible and no Sacraments without the Church and the *ministerium ecclesiasticum.*'[2]

The third mark of the Church is that its corporate life is new life. To live in the Spirit means to be redeemed from the clutches of this present evil world and to walk in newness of life. This can only mean newness of social life, since there is no other kind of human life. If our faith is not indefeasibly social we are walking in craftiness and handling the Word of God deceitfully. The worst blasphemy is that of an unethical evangelicalism: it is what the sin against the Holy Ghost really means.

Christian people in every generation have never doubted this the implicit logic of the Gospel. God's holy will has to be done, even here in Babylon. Holy Scripture will never allow us to make any mistake about this; nor will Church History. There is no other way of knowing God than by responding to

[1] *W.A.* vi. p. 530.

[2] Quoted by O. Piper, *Gotteswahrheit und die Wahrheit der Kirche,* p. 17.

his claims upon us; and his claims are made here, just where we live. To attempt to evade this in quietist fashion, would be to throw the Bible into the dustbin. It would be to cut ourselves off from the witness of the Holy Spirit in the Church, as he spoke by the Prophets, and as he has spoken to the heart of an Aquinas, a Calvin, a Richard Baxter, a Thomas Chalmers, a Charles Gore. The Gospel can never be unethical without ceasing to be the Gospel. From beginning to end it is concerned with moral realities, and therefore with time, and with this strange world of necessity and freedom wherein God has set us, to live our life to his glory.

Here again, we feel the same tension between the individual and the corporate which we have been feeling all along. The Christian has two different problems to tackle here. There is, first and always, the problem of his own personal responsibility to God. 'Hier steh ich.' But, secondly, as a member of a corporate body, the community, he has to ask what is the right policy and decision for the common enterprise in which he is engaged with others. These two problems are distinct, though obviously related. If I may say so, it is one of the merits of Dr Oldham's *Christian News-Letter* that he makes Christians feel the complexity as well as the urgency of their common ethical problems, thanks to this dialectical tension. 'Many people either think almost exclusively in terms of the personal responsibility of the individual Christian and ignore the other quite different problem of corporate activities and the working of institutions. Or, alternatively, they resolve Christianity into a programme for the improvement of the collective life and forget the profound inner transformation which it demands from men and the heights of perfection to which it summons them.'[1]

[1] *Christian News-Letter*, No. 9.

The tension between these two truths, each of which demands active recognition from Christ's Church on earth, constitutes the peculiar problem of Christian social ethics. Modern realism in theology rightly repudiates the social idealism which would claim to be the sum and substance of the Gospel. A human society which has been forced by events to rediscover the exceeding sinfulness of sin, has also rediscovered that faith in man is the worship of an idol with feet of clay. Blue prints for Utopia are certainly discredited. No modern theologian has done more to recover this note of realism than Reinhold Niebuhr. We do well to heed his complementary warning, therefore, that Christians should beware of accepting the habits of a sinful world as the norm for their collective life. Frequently Christians are tempted by their recognition of the sinfulness of human existence to disavow their own responsibility for a tolerable social justice.

The tension remains and will remain. Only by living here and now in the eternal world are we able to live effectively in this fallen world to the glory of God. Only as we look for his Kingdom beyond time and death and the fashion of this world that passeth away, are we able to pray and work for this world, saying 'Thy Kingdom come'. Only as we worship are we able effectively to work. The Church in its worship praises God for the means of grace, and for the hope of glory. These two great themes form the climax, therefore, in any systematic account of Christian doctrine. We turn to them in the two concluding lectures.

Additional Note to Lecture VI

THE REFORMATION AND CHURCHMANSHIP

No misunderstanding of the Reformation is more pathetic and no misrepresentation of it more perverse, than the contention that it had no essential interest in Churchmanship, as traditional and authoritative. The ignorant, and this includes many whose ignorance is inexcusable, still persist in speaking of 'Protestant Individualism', as though Luther and Calvin were not great High Churchmen, but peevish little individualists shut up in the dungeons of their own subjectivism.

(i) *Luther*. It is deplorable that the learned Whitney, for example, who knew so much about Lutheranism in its politico-ecclesiastical aspect, was so little interested in Luther's religion and so ignorant of its theological expression in volume after volume of the *Weimar Ausgabe*. To be content with '*Wace and Buchheim*' in 1939 is to betray contempt for the *Lutherforschung* of the past fifty years. In Whitney's *Reformation Essays* the old clichés are repeated, unsupported by any evidence, that Luther made himself the symbol of the individual conscience and of individual liberty (pp. 36 and 112), and that he 'underestimated the value of good works' and 'really cared little for the Church' (p. 78). One wonders how a historian with any knowledge of what Luther actually wrote could be content with the repetition of errors so stale. Even the Romans are now more cautious, as a volume such as *Luther in ökumenischer Sicht* (ed. Martin, Stuttgart, 1929) testifies. The first-rate research of German, French and American scholars has long since registered a reaction against the too-triumphant onslaught of

Denifle and Grisar. No one may read Seeberg's volume on Luther in the second edition of his great *Dogmengeschichte* (IV), nor Karl Holl's *Gesammelte Aufsätze* (I) without realizing that the classic theology of continental Protestantism is largely unknown country to Anglican writers of a certain school, whose cheap attacks recall Newman at his worst, and represent neither malice nor ignorance, but both. Two points call for notice here.

(*a*) The first is made by Otto Piper in his *God in History* (p. 155): 'At the moment when the Occident seemed to be disintegrating completely and irreparably, the Reformers stepped into the breach and restored its unity. Roman Catholic and Anglican writers frequently blame the Reformation for destroying the unity of mediaeval Europe. They overlook, however, that that unity had actually broken down more than one hundred and fifty years before. In the fifteenth century the Roman Catholic Church not only was no longer capable of repressing the growing nationalism, but also was deeply involved itself in the rivalries of national groups. Moreover, the opponents of Protestantism underrate the harmful effects of the Renaissance... a movement aiming at delivering secular life from supra-natural bondages. This strife for independence, if left to itself, would have rushed Europe into chaos. As Nietzsche rightly observed, it was Luther who curbed its growth.'

(*b*) The second point demanding notice is that Luther, like St Paul, was never weary of enunciating the self-evident truth of the Gospel; namely that *glauben* and *lieben* are correlatives. Faith without ethical consequences is a lie. Good works must necessarily follow faith. God does not need our sacrifices but he has, nevertheless, appointed a representative to receive them, namely, our neighbour. The neighbour always represents the invisible Christ.

To insist on this familiar fact is not to deny that Lutheranism has sometimes been in danger of quietism; the Lutheran ethic was not unaffected by its strong eschatological interest. Nevertheless, it would be an absurd caricature of the Lutheran system to omit or belittle its emphasis on sanctification as an abiding process in the Church, complementary to the finished work of creation and redemption. The Holy Spirit governs the Church (Spiritus Rector) through the Word and the Sacraments; his work goes on until the Last Judgment, since our sanctification is ever imperfect in this world. Indeed, Luther includes sanctification in the process of justification; only a generation which has forgotten the scriptural meaning of eschatology will misunderstand him. Even Calvinism, with its more active piety and its stronger emphasis on the social ethic, has been interpreted as *meditatio futurae vitae* (Schulze).

(ii) *Calvin.* It is deplorable, too, that Dr Prestige's last book, to which I would again pay my grateful tribute, should be marred by a calumny on Calvin which is almost comic in its downright error. On pp. 404–5 of *Fathers and Heretics* we read that 'Calvin demanded of his followers a clean breach with historic Christendom', a breach which was complete in devotion as well as in doctrine. 'He treats of the tremendous themes of Christ's manhood and of man's redemption without a trace of unction; these subjects seem to stir his feelings no more profoundly than the compilation of a series of trade returns might excite the bosom of a government clerk.' When I first came upon these words I had just been spending some hours on the *Summa Theologica* of Thomas Aquinas, and I could not help reflecting that anyone who had not been trained to distinguish between formal theology and devotional homiletics might make the same querulous and foolish criticism of the great doctor and saint of the thirteenth century. There are fifty-eight volumes of Calvin's work in the great Strasburg edition; and even the two most famous and most often consulted of these, the *Institutio*, can hardly take the place of Commentaries, Theological Tractates, Catechisms, Confessions of Faith, Letters, Ecclesiastical Ordinances and Prayers, if Dr Prestige's statements are to be tested by evidence. But even so, the evidence of the *Institutio* (last and definitive edition) is enough to substantiate the findings of a score of modern scholars (Peter Barth, Bohatec, Mulhaupt, Wernle, Doumergue, Holl, A. Lang, N. Weiss, Niesel and Bauke, to name only these), namely that Calvin's massive theological and ecclesiological system is not a clean breach with historic Christendom, but a structure resting on Holy Scripture and ancient ecclesiastical usage. Calvin's championship of ancient catholic usage during the first five centuries, 'ante papatum', is well known (cf. I. 13. 3f.; II. 16. 5; IV. 9. 8). It is of the first five centuries that he says 'magis adhuc florebat religio et sincerior doctrina vigebat' (I. xi. 13). Calvin asserts, naturally enough, that when God does not prescribe any fixed rule for us in his Word, the conscience must not be burdened with traditional practices (III. 4. 12); yet he saw the significance of tradition and rated it highly (II. 2. 7). He begins his constructive work in Geneva (see the *Ordonnances Ecclésiastiques*) by asking 'quid ex antiquitate restituendum' and 'quis fuerit olim verus usus ecclesiasticae jurisdictionis?' He asks such questions because (as Book IV of the *Institutio* makes clear) Christ has willed to rule his Church, not directly and in person, but through institutions made known to us through the Scriptures and preserved in the constitution of the apostolic and old catholic church, itself a constitutive part of God's revelation to men. There is much, says Calvin, in the customary life of the Church 'quorum nec tempus nec modus nec forma praescribitur verbo Dei sed in ecclesiae judicio relinquitur'. The reply to Sadolet (*Op.* v. 394) is entirely in line with *Op.* x a. 15, 93. Calvin's churchmanship rests not only on the evidence of the Scriptures, but on the history of the Church. (See his letter to Farel on ancient Catholic usage, *Op.* xi. 281; cf. also *Op.* i. 561, 567 = ii. 776, 782.) He appeals constantly to Augustine and Chrysostom; to Cyprian, Jerome and Gregory. Indeed, next to Augustine, his most frequent appeal in the *Institutio* is to Bernard of Clairvaux; and even so, not to the *De Consideratione* (as might perhaps have been expected) where Bernard lashes the vices of the mediaeval church; but to that faith, evangelical and catholic, which is expounded in his *Sermons on the Canticles*. Dr Prestige says much about St Bernard in his valuable book, much that is severely critical. That Calvin should quote St Bernard so often and with approval is a strange comment on his 'clean breach with historic Christendom'.

Further, this very charge is refuted by Calvin himself in more than one place. 'Je ne suis pas tant aspre, ne tant extreme de vouloir interdire du tout et sans exception a l'homme chrestien, qu'il n'ait a se conformer avec les papistes en aucune ceremonie ou observation. Car je n'entens de condamner sinon ce qui est pleinement mauvais et appertement vitieux' (*Op.* vi. 522). He is careful to remind his readers that the elect are found within the Roman church (*Op.* vi. 583) and that it has preserved remnants of real Christianity (*Op.* xb. 149; xiii. 308, 487). He grants, too, that in theory everything in that church is referred to divine grace (*Op.* v. 411 and vi. 461). He recognizes that the veneration of saints is well-intentioned (*Op.* VI. 409). Moreover, it gives him no pleasure to expose the vices of mediaeval Catholicism ('equidem nec traducendis eorum vitiis delector', *Op.* VI. 470).

Calvin's lifelong desire to restore the ancient practice of weekly communion for all the people explains his breach with the mediaeval custom of lay communion only once or twice a year, which he describes as a 'diabolic invention'. He wanted a celebration (with full participation of course), at least once a week ('singulis ad minimum hebdomadibus'; *Articles* of 1537). In this reform, as in much else, he is more in line with the Oxford Movement than is always realized.

VII

THE MEANS OF GRACE

THE CHRISTIAN DOCTRINE OF THE WORD
AND THE SACRAMENTS

I F Cambridge were a continental University, we should all
be regarded as a special social class, and labelled as such:
'Students'. The word suggests that intellectual activities
are a specialized function. Some men are policemen or poets
or even politicians, but we are students. We attend lectures,
study prescribed books and pass examinations.

This idea is amusing and even annoying for one main reason.
It isolates thought from life and fosters mere intellectualism.
Every science is necessarily an abstraction from the whole
content of reality. Merely to study, say, Political Science,
Natural Science or Theology the Queen of Sciences would be
like knowing all about the off-side rule, but never playing
football. It would be as unreal as hanging a large-scale map of
Cambridge and district in one's rooms, but never doing even
the Grantchester Grind. What Alexander Pope said about the
study of Biology is true of all the sciences, all purely academic
study:

'Like following life through creatures you dissect,
You lose it in the moment you detect.'

This selective character of the sciences is essential to their
progress, admittedly, but it limits their scope. In short, as
'students' we are all inevitably concerned with analysis and

measurement; we work out our formulae. But formulae have a smaller content than actual experience. There is a wholeness about Reality, which makes our reflective apprehension of it a partial thing. Unless we take care, the living subject-matter disintegrates as we handle it, and we are left with dry bones.[1]

This danger is nowhere more acute than in the study of theology. Indeed, one of the perils always threatening the religious life is that people get 'interested' in it, and begin to study it. They even go to lectures on Christian Doctrine. More dangerous still, they may go to special colleges and become students of theology, not fully realizing that reading books about God, so far from leading a man to the knowledge of God, may have the opposite effect. You may spend years on the sacred texts, the wearisome minutiae of linguistic and archaeological research, the arguments about the deepest things by which men have lived. But by studying these facts it is easy to lose the life which alone gives them unity and meaning. Nowhere is the need for synthesis as great as here. Here, as nowhere else, the 'student' longs for objectivity. The mind may labour with great concepts such as that of the Trinity in unity, but the whole man cries out for the living God. As Luther put it in a striking epigram: 'He who merely studies the commandments of God (*mandata Dei*) is not greatly moved. But he who listens to God commanding (*Deum mandantem*), how can he fail to be terrified by majesty so great?'[2]

[1] There is no more perfect expression of this in literature than the first hundred lines of Goethe's *Faust*, Part i:

> 'Statt der lebendigen Natur
> Da Gott die Menschen schuf hinein,
> Umgibt in Rauch und Moder nur
> Dich Tiergeripp und Totenbein.'

[2] *W.A.* iv. 305.

We have to get somehow from *mandata Dei* to *Deus mandans* if our study of Christian doctrine is to mean anything vital. We want a living synthesis where those very facts, which the intellect dissects and coldly examines, are given back to us with the wholeness which belongs to life. If this need for integration is not met, we are no better than children in the nursery playing 'Church'. We have, as Valentine said of Thurio, 'an exchequer of words, but no other treasure'. Instead of putting off our shoes from our feet because the place whereon we stand is holy ground, we are taking nice photographs of the burning Bush, from suitable angles: we are chatting about theories of Atonement with our feet on the mantelpiece, instead of kneeling down before the wounds of Christ.

The need is obvious. Is it met anywhere? The answer is that it is met in the worship of the Church, where the Christian religion is given to us in all its living meaning. Apart from this, Christianity is no more than archaeology, a museum piece for antiquarians. The Church lives, not on ideas about God, but on God's grace itself, mediated by his Spirit through the immemorial rites of corporate worship. There the Word of God, contained in the words of Holy Scripture, is proclaimed and heard as the Gospel. There in the Sacrament of the Eucharist, this Word reaches its climax, and action adds something to utterance.

'One of the clearest results of all religious history and religious psychology', said Troeltsch, 'is that the essence of all Religion is not the Dogma and Idea, but the Cultus and Communion; the living intercourse with God, an intercourse of the entire community, having its vital roots in religion and deriving its ultimate power of thus conjoining individuals, from its faith in God.' In short, saving faith comes to men not through any intellectual gymnastics of their own; it is wrought by the Holy Spirit of God in the heart through the preaching of the Gospel; the same Holy Spirit confirms or seals it through the Gospel Sacraments.

Thus, in the full diet of public worship in every Church throughout Christendom, two permanent elements together constitute 'the means of grace'; first, the preaching and hearing of the Word; second, the Sacrament of the Eucharist, where the highest is not spoken but acted; where the promises of the Gospel are visibly sealed by the Yea and Amen of a ritual act. Separable though they may be in our practice, these two elements are one service in our thought. They are the two foci of an ellipse, together forming a unity to which each is equally indispensable. Differing in their operation they are one in their essential function, which is the publication of the Gospel of Redemption in all its incomparable majesty and comfort. Whatever the rich variety of its historic forms Christian worship has always and everywhere received the blessing of the Gospel in this two-fold way of Christ's appointing.

The preaching of the Word: what, in brief, does it mean? Woe is me if I preach not the Gospel, says the greatest of the Apostles. The New Testament speaks with the same urgency and high confidence, because the greatest of human concerns is salvation. The Gospel is not a book but a living Word, which God himself cries aloud to all the world using as his mouthpiece those whom he calls to be his ministers. 'God's Word', says Calvin, 'is uttered by men like ourselves; common men who may even be much inferior to us in dignity and social importance. But when some insignificant little man (*homuncio quispiam*) is raised up out of the dust to speak God's Word, he is God's own minister,'[1] God's very lieutenant. The preaching of the Word of God is the Word of God.

[1] *Inst.* IV. iii. 1.

Thus the preacher of the Word is more than a historian. He is a herald. He is no mere lecturer stimulating interest in the past, but an evangelist whose vocation and responsibility it is to cry 'This day is this scripture fulfilled in your ears...now is the accepted time'. The herald is not sent to deliver his own soul, but to preach the glorious gospel of the blessed God. He is a King's Messenger, no more and no less. The vitality of his message does not depend on him, or on his character; he may be a bad man. Nevertheless, says St Paul, Christ is preached. All Christian preaching finds its only sanction and power in the authority of a human life, death and resurrection through which God spoke in the fulness of time, and through which, by his Spirit in the Church, he speaks so long as time endures.

Let me repeat; the Word and the Sacraments make one indissoluble unity. The Pulpit and the Holy Table, Sermon and Eucharist, are means of grace provided for us from the very beginning of Christian history. The preached Word of the Gospel comes to its own climax in the visible Word of the Eucharist. Similarly, the Eucharist presupposes the preached Word of the Gospel; it is the sacred pledge and seal of the promises of God, just as the seal at the foot of parchment implies the precious covenant of which it is the guarantee, and without which it would be meaningless. The preaching of the Gospel and the administration of the Gospel Sacraments are of Christ's institution: to exalt one above the other would be to disobey him whose means of grace they are. I spoke just now of an ellipse with two foci: it would be more accurate to speak of two circles having a common centre. Here is the focal centre of the Church's undying life. Here, too, the life of God's people in every generation is integrated as One Body. The

Jesus whose words and works you may have studied in books, and whom you may have sought to understand through the classic formulae of Christian doctrine, here rises from the dead. Here the grave clothes of academic theology are neatly folded and put on one side. He is not entombed, either in history or in scholastic philosophy; he is risen. He is known of us in the breaking of Bread.

We come, then, to the Gospel Sacraments, their origin, nature and meaning.

First, as to their origin. Some will tell you that Sacraments originate in our need of them; which is true but misleading here. We do need symbols to compass the ineffable things of our experience. Goethe went to the root of this matter when he said that the highest cannot be spoken: it can only be acted. The inadequacy of words, the impotence of definitions is notorious. You may remember that Joe Vance always regarded Beethoven not only as a composer but as a revelation. 'His music always seemed to express everything that I can understand and to supply exhaustive conclusions in all the crucial questions of life and death.... How often I said to myself after some perfectly convincing phrase of Beethoven, "of course, if that is so, there is no occasion to worry". It could not be translated, naturally, into vulgar grammar and syntax, but it left no doubt on the point for all that.'

Joe Vance there speaks for many, and though his speech is extravagant, it does illustrate the fact that ideas, of which words are the clothing, cannot express all that we experience. That 'perfectly convincing phrase' was not made up of words, but of music. Great art needs no wordy explanations. It is in the music itself, in great pictures, great drama, great institutions embodying ethical ideas, that language is transcended. The symbolism is never the same for all, of course: for one it is a canvas by Raphael, for another it is 'the meanest flower that blows'. But for all, the Eternal may be seen in and through these temporal things, these outward signs of an inward and spiritual grace,

> When on some gilded cloud, or flower,
> My gazing soul would dwell an hour,
> And in those weaker glories spy
> Some shadows of eternity.

All this, let me repeat, is not untrue: moreover, it is a sound inference from the Christian doctrine of Creation, as St Augustine insisted. This is what people mean when they say that the Universe is 'sacramental'; that this world is the garment of the invisible God, the Soul of Reality who thus speaks to man, saying 'Hoc est corpus meum'.

But this is no true account of the Gospel Sacraments. In these symbols of bread and wine, the whole meaning of our religion comes to its focus and is made plain. But why *these* symbols? Why not anything arbitrarily chosen from the common stock, after the manner of Mysticism? Why not gilded cloud or flower? For Wordsworth the meanest flower that blows sufficed. Why, then, should not Christians choose—not just anything, but some great things—a *Mass in B minor*, a Sistine Madonna, a Passion Play at Oberammergau, a Parable like that of the Prodigal Son—to symbolize the ineffable deeps of religious experience?

The answer, as we have been reminding ourselves throughout these lectures, is that the Christian Revelation is rooted in history. The Gospel is a Gospel of Divine Action in time. We do not choose the symbols of water, bread and wine. They are chosen for us, given to us: these rites of Baptism and Eucharist go back to Christ himself. There is nothing older than this in Christendom. Before theology; before all our ecclesiasticism; before ever a word of the New Testament was written, this was. This is the earliest Gospel. Indeed, it is rooted in the immemorial covenant which God made with his people Israel. We take Bread and we take the Cup because the Redeemer himself is the fountain head of this living tradition. *Ipse Dominus fecit.* The Christian is born into an evangelical context, an historical heritage to which certain facts belong constitutively and for ever, namely the Commandments, the Beatitudes, the Lord's Prayer; a manger at Bethlehem; a Cross on Calvary; a broken body; an outpoured life; the Bread and the Wine. These things are not ours to accept or reject; they are there from the foundation of the world.

Go back to Goethe for a moment: 'The highest cannot be spoken; it can only be acted.' Well, the supreme Christian Sacrament is a drama. As often as we eat the Bread and drink the Cup we do show forth the dying of the Lord Jesus; we do re-enact the drama, which thus exhibits, truly and efficaciously, the mystery of our Redemption as no theology of Atonement has ever been able to do. This is our Symbol because he said: 'Do this in remembrance of me.'

Moreover, Christian men have done this ever since. Even if this rite meant little to us and made no living claim on our devotion, we should still have to account for its abiding energy in the life of the Church. It lasts because it speaks a universal, eternal word. Other symbols there certainly are, having their local, temporary significance. I have already mentioned three or four which move us deeply. But even so we cannot all go to

Dresden to see Raphael's Madonna. Bach's *Mass* may 'dissolve me into ecstasies, and bring all heaven before mine eyes', but it is not everybody's symbol. Oberammergau is a spectacle provided for the relatively few, once in ten years. Even the Parable of the Prodigal does not sum up all that is vital to the Christian faith. The very particularity of such symbolism separates it from the timeless simplicity and universality of water and bread and wine. Men have attempted to improve on the institution of Christ, often with the best motives. The evidence of the catacombs suggests that the Eucharist of the early Church was sometimes celebrated with fish, in memory of that eucharistic meal when Christ fed five thousand. The Kollyridians of the fourth century used something like cheese-cakes. Much later the Frisian Mennonites practised mutual feet-washing, taking the moving words of St John xiii to be a holy ordinance of Christ (*ritus praeceptus*). The Greek and Roman Churches reckon seven sacraments, that is, Baptism, Confirmation, Eucharist, Penance, Extreme Unction, Orders, Marriage. Yet, even so, the Roman Church does not attribute an equal dignity to all seven: three only have an indelible character and may on no account be repeated, namely Baptism, Confirmation and Orders (a sound practice at any rate, with which no Christian could disagree). But the sounder doctrine of the Thirty-nine Articles, and of Protestantism generally, limits the true Christian sacraments to the two visible signs or ceremonies, instituted by Christ himself.[1] As soon as we begin speaking of other sacraments beside the two given to us in the Gospels, a dangerous subjectivism threatens the historic faith. There is no limiting the number of such so-called sacraments. The Scholastics of the Middle Ages

[1] Cf. *Conf. Belg.* Art. 35.

enumerated thirty at different times,[1] and our modern interest in symbolism is ready to make the whole of nature symbolic, with the result that Sacraments in the Christian sense are destroyed. Baptism and the Lord's Supper are means of grace. They are, as Augustine put it, visible words[2] exhibiting with a moving actuality what has been received of the Lord, and continuously delivered to the whole company of the redeemed in every generation.

In the second place, what is the nature and meaning of these means of grace? The word 'symbol' may easily mislead us. The Swastika is the symbol of the Nazis. Or, to use a happier illustration, a primrose is symbolic of spring; but the Church means something different by the word 'Sacrament', because it means something more than a mere token or sign. In the ancient world a symbol was always, in some sense, the thing it symbolized. And there is no ecclesiastical confession in Christendom which does not insist that the Sacraments, as a Swiss Declaration puts it,[3] are never bare signs or mere illustrations, 'nuda, vacua, inania signa'. To use a classic expression, the Eucharist is a *signum efficax*; that is, it is a sign which verily effects something: it conveys what it signifies, namely the grace of Christ's finished work. The Sacraments do not add anything to the Word, any more than the kiss and the ring add anything to plighted troth. But they do movingly reiterate it; they give effect to it. 'They be certain sure witnesses and effectual signs of grace, and God's good will

---

[1] Cf. O. Fricke, *Die Sakramente in der Protestantischen Kirche*, p. 25.

[2] *Contra Faustum*, xix. 16. Cf. *de catechizandis rudibus* xxvi. 50: 'signacula quidem rerum divinarum esse visibilia, sed res ipsas invisibiles in eis honorari.'

[3] *Declar. Thor.* p. 61.

towards us, by the which he doth work invisibly in us, and doth not only quicken but also strengthen our Faith in him.' These familiar words from the Thirty-nine Articles, closely based on the Augsburg Confession, testify that the Sacraments do verily mediate God's grace. They are more than mere remembrances of heavenly things; the Church would be capable of such remembrance without Sacraments. They are signs whereby the Holy Spirit inwardly affects us. Like the printed score of the *Fifth Symphony*, through which the music in Beethoven's mind is mediated to successive generations, so the Sacraments are 'conveyances'; sign and effect coincide; the score is played and the music heard; so, God himself sacramentally unites the symbolic action and the grace which it conveys.

In short the emphasis here is always on God and his action. 'Prayer is a gift and a sacrifice that we make: Sacrament is a gift and a sacrifice that God makes. In prayer we go to God: in Sacrament God comes to us.'[1] The essential fact in the Eucharist is not man's remembrance and commemoration of Christ's death, but the fact that Christ here gives himself to man. If Sacraments are really important for our salvation, and the Church has never doubted that they are, their efficacy must have a basis independent of man. It is Christ himself, therefore, who administers the Sacraments. They are his, remember: not mine, or yours. He invites us to his Table. He is *hospes atque epulum*, that is, the Giver of the Feast as well as the Feast itself. Ordination does not mean that the priest or minister has now a higher rank than ordinary Christians and is able to minister instead of Christ. The Sacraments are efficacious only because

[1] P. T. Forsyth, quoted by N. Micklem, *Christian Worship, Studies in its history and meaning*, by members of Mansfield College (Oxford, 1936).

Christ himself uses the minister as his instrument. In short, vital to all Sacraments is God's action, not the priest's action.

This means something more. The efficacy of Sacraments cannot depend on the character and qualities of the man who administers them. The validity of the Sacrament is not destroyed because it has been celebrated by a man whose life is quite immoral or who has no faith at all. I am here postulating a situation scandalous and hurtful in the extreme, though by no means impossible. My point is that the character of the ministrant is strictly irrelevant. If it were not so, the Sacraments could never be celebrated at all, since all Christ's ministers are sinners. No man is ever good enough to 'be put in trust' with the Gospel, to be 'a steward of the Mysteries'. As the *Westminster Confession* has it: 'Neither does the efficacy of a Sacrament depend upon the piety or intention of him that doth administer it, but upon the Work of the Spirit and the Word of Institution' (xxvii. 3).

One vital question remains to be considered here; namely, on what does the operation of the Sacraments depend? Not on the ministrant, as we have already seen. Or, to use a technical expression which can hardly be bettered, not *ex opere operantis*. That is, it does not depend on what the celebrant, as such, does. The main thing is not the sacramental action in its manward aspect, but in its Godward aspect. In the Sacraments we have effectual signs of God acting.

Would it be sound doctrine, then, to teach, as Rome does, that the Sacraments exert their influence *ex opere operato*, that is, simply through the objective performance of the rite? (Just as inoculation exerts its influence on a man's body, irrespective of his feelings about it; he may be asleep or unconscious while it does its healing work: or just as a fire warms simply by the fact of our coming to stand in front of it; the burning coal is the *opus operatum*, and our bodily presence is alone necessary to make its warmth operative.) Do these analogies fairly describe the operation of the Sacraments in any sense? The answer is that they do: yet the answer may be made in so crude a way that it would be truer to say that they do not. Let me say two things in elucidation.

First, it is erroneous to suppose that Protestantism repudiates this great truth as to the objective operation and efficacy of the Gospel Sacraments. It is also misleading to say that Roman doctrine requires no faith at all from the recipient of the Sacraments. To quote Cardinal Bellarmine: 'Goodwill, faith and penitence are necessary in the adult communicant, not as the active cause of sacramental grace, nor as giving efficacy to the Sacrament. These dispositions merely remove the obstacles which might hinder its efficacy.'[1] Now, no Protestant would deny this, even though he means by 'faith' something notably different from what this great Jesuit meant. Indeed, the classic Protestant Confessions do not deny this, but they go much further.

Secondly, then, Protestantism has never even distantly denied that God's power dwells in the Sacraments in virtue of the Lord's institution. But it denies that grace is ever conferred *ex opere operato* without corresponding faith on the part of the recipient. The grace of the Gospel is not a 'thing', a sort of spiritual 'blood-plasm' for distribution to men through the channels of the sacramental system: a divine 'stuff', so to

---

[1] *De Sacram.* II. i: 'non ut causae activae, non enim fides et poenitentia efficiunt gratiam sacramentalem neque dant efficaciam sacramenti, sed solum tollunt obstacula, quae impedirent, ne sacramenta suam efficaciam exercere possent....'

speak, fused indissolubly with the sacramental elements, and working in magically objective fashion on the soul of the Communicant, without conscious response on his part, just as aspirin might work on his body. In a famous sentence of three words, St Augustine said: 'Believe and thou hast eaten of the Sacraments' (crede et manducasti).[1] He meant that faith in God's action is the ultimate requisite here. The grace of God is mediated not so much through faith as to faith. A grossly realistic objectivism here easily degenerates into superstition, as the history of the Church makes only too plain. This may be avoided only in one way. We have to remember that the Sacraments derive their whole meaning from the redeeming *Work* of Christ, if I may put it so, rather than from his *Essence*. The heart of the Sacrament is divine Action not divine Substance. God's grace is conveyed not through the elements but through the act. As my friend Nathaniel Micklem has put it: 'The efficacy of Baptism is not in water, but in washing: of the Communion, not in bread but in bread broken. The elements are as integral to the Sacrament as the words to the sentence; but as it is the whole sentence alone which is effectual as conveying meaning, so it is the Word (and not the elements) that conveys grace in the Sacrament.'[2]

Nothing illustrates the Christian doctrine of the Sacraments so unambiguously as the Sacrament of Baptism. For here the recipient of the Sacrament is, usually, not an adult but a tiny infant. Thus, some of the issues which we have been considering are here presented at their sharpest.

[1] *In Joh.* xxv. 12. Cf. *Ibid.* xxvi. 1, xxxv. 3. But see Seeberg, *DG*[2]. II. 460.
[2] *Christian Worship* .p. 245.

Let me remind you of the main issue. We met it when considering the doctrine of the Church, and we have met it again here. To use two clumsy and overworked yet useful words, it is the issue between the objective and the subjective in religion. Where is the accent, the main emphasis to be put in Christian doctrine? On the believer, or on God? Does it fall on our personal faith, our self-dedication, our fellowship, our moral idealism and moral achievements, or does it fall rather on the divine initiative; what God has done, the objective fact that God in Christ has redeemed men? Is the Church merely a number of local associations of believers, or is it something more; an undying Institution which is supra-personal and supra-temporal?

Obviously the answer is that both statements are true. We may not say 'Either...Or' here. God acts redemptively through his Church and his Sacraments: man responds by faith. Therefore Christian doctrine has always to be ready to fight on two fronts: against an excessive subjectivism on the one hand, which tends to belittle the Corporate, the Institutional, the Objective; and against an excessive objectivism on the other hand, which would underestimate the personal individual, intimate elements in all true religion.

Now the Sacrament of Baptism, administered almost exclusively to infants, and unrepeatable, obviously emphasizes the objective givenness of the Gospel of Redemption. Christ has redeemed all mankind, and the divinely given sign of this fact is baptism. It proclaims that Christ has done something for me, without ever consulting me or waiting for my approval; before ever I was born or thought of he died to redeem me. His Cross is not merely a moral appeal which may influence me; it is a fact in time where something was done for ever, to reconcile me and all other sinners to God. When Luther was most afflicted with temptations and doubts he would write two words on his table with a piece of chalk: *Baptizatus sum* (I have been baptized). He meant that baptism was the foundation of his Christian certainty. In the fact that he was baptized before he had any knowledge of salvation or any desire for it, God teaches him that the divine mercy sought him independently of his attitude towards God.

The significance of infant baptism is thus three-fold:

First, it guards against the menace of mere subjectivism. The great and world-wide denomination of Baptists is so named because its members rightly insist that to be a Christian a man or woman must be a believer. The faith must be his or her personal affair. Thus the Baptists recognize no other baptism than that which they administer to candidates who have reached years of discretion. They argue that to baptize a help-less infant only a few weeks old, who is obviously incapable of the responsive faith of the believer, is meaningless and worse. To this the universal tradition of Christendom replies, not of course by belittling personal faith in an adult who seeks baptism, but by insisting on our redemption as an objective fact just at that point in human life where no subjective re-sponse to it is possible on the part of the baptized individual.

In the second place, infant baptism guards against the irrelevant fancy known as 'dedicatory baptism', whereby parents who know no better suppose that in this rite they are dedicating the child to God. It is doubtless true that they are doing so, but compared with the main fact, the declaration of what Christ has done for this child on Calvary, such dedication is neither here nor there. The rite of baptism would, strictly speaking, be superfluous if it signified no more than an offering of the child by his parents to God. Such offering is doubtless good, but it is secondary here. Here, with the water of cleansing as the God-given sign, the Church proclaims the primary fact: namely, that God loves this child, and Christ died that it might be incorporate in the great company of his redeemed.

In the third place, the practice and the doctrine of infant baptism has been and is the great historical guarantee of the Church as something more than loose local associations of believers. This Sacrament is one of the foundation stones of the Church Institutional, Oecumenical and Corporate, a great supra-temporal fact in the heart of God. You perceive the difficulty, I think. No sacramental act achieves anything unless it corresponds to what happens in experience. Thus baptism has no efficacy apart from faith. Is infant baptism, then, the most blatant instance of *opus operatum*? The answer is that the faith is that of the Church, not of the child. Baptism is a real act of the Church and, therefore, of Christ. He it is who takes the child in his arms and declares what he has done and will do for it. Baptism is neither an act of dedication in which the main thing is what the celebrants do; nor is it a magic rite effecting regeneration. The child is baptized by Christ into his Church, the household of faith.

From this act of Christ in his Church we turn to the real presence of Christ in the Eucharist or the Lord's Supper, which is the other great Gospel Sacrament. What does this real presence mean?

The Eucharist has many aspects, and even if we could describe them all, the rite would still transcend our explanation. A sacrament which could be analysed into concepts would cease to be a sacrament. But there are three aspects of the Eucharist which may well concern us here:

The first is its historical or memorial aspect. The Holy Table represents a direct and unbroken historical continuity with Christian origins. It is a fact that not a single Sunday morning has passed since the first Holy Week, without Christians meeting at this Table. What is said and done here formed the earliest deposit of a Christian tradition which has never lapsed. Here we do not read something out of the records of the historic past, even though those records be the most precious books in the world, the Gospels. We remember something earlier than the written Gospels. The mysterious life of the Church is continuously renewed through its unbroken remembrance and dramatic repetition of certain mysterious words and acts of our Saviour, on the night in which he was betrayed. This past is no mere past. The supreme events of the life of Jesus, continuously remembered, are a present fact.

Secondly, our remembrance is expressed in action, in the manual acts of breaking the bread and taking the cup, of eating and drinking together in the ritual meal of Holy Communion. But, as you will remember from what I said in my fourth lecture, on Christ Crucified, there is no meaning in this meal except as the last stage of sacrifice. Just as our physical life is sustained only because the wheat falls into the ground and dies for us, and the grape yields up its life-blood for us,[1] so the Bread and Wine are the effective signs of our spiritual sustenance at the Table of him who is both our Victim, our High Priest and our Food. He is the Bread of life sent down from heaven, and broken for us. 'To us', says the earliest

---

[1] Fricke, *op. cit.* p. 38: 'Alle Nahrung ist geopfertes Leben.'

extant liturgy of the Church, the Didache, 'thou hast given spiritual food and drink through thy Servant.'[1]

The Servant is the Lamb of God who comes with us as we draw near to the Altar of God. He makes himself one with us in the Incarnation. We sinners kill our Victim; the Crucified takes his blood, his surrendered, outpoured life, now our life through our identification with him, through the veil of his broken flesh into God's very presence. He atones for us. In the offering of his Manhood, our separate manhoods conjoined with his, are also offered to God in eternal service. God accepts the offering by the fire of his Spirit, and so transforms it. Thus, does he receive us at his Board, the Table of the Lord which is the earthly image of the heavenly Altar. The very life of God, the Creator and the Redeemer, is here made available to us, through the Holy Spirit. We celebrate the mystery of life as corporate communion in and with the eternal God.

This is the second aspect of the Eucharist, its timeless or eternal aspect. The Feast mediates to us God's presence and his very Self.

In the third place, these two aspects here fuse into one. At this Table there is a unique synthesis of what is historical and what is beyond history. Through the remembered events of time the Church experiences the timeless presence of Christ. 'Past, present and future', says Professor Dodd, 'are indissolubly united in the Sacrament. It may be regarded as a dramatization of the advent of the Lord, which is at once his remembered coming in humiliation and his desired coming in glory, both realized in his true presence in the Sacrament.'[2] Thus, we know two things with certainty in this Sacrament.

---

[1] x. 3. Cf. also ix. 2-3.   [2] *The Apostolic Preaching*, p. 234.

First, Jesus Christ is not merely a figure of the historic past who is remembered because he is admired (like Isaiah, Epictetus or Boethius). He is the eternal Word, Bread from Heaven given to believers in every generation as the promise and foretaste of the Messianic feast in the Kingdom of God. The Eucharist lifts us, earth bound and time bound as we are, into 'the Heavenlies'. Here the temporal is known as eternal.

But secondly, the living God whom we worship is not adequately described as *ens realissimum* or as an impersonal Absolute transcending history. He is God revealed to us in Christ. Christian worship differs from Christian theism in that the Incarnation makes God real and present to us. Here the eternal is known as temporal.

In short, the Incarnation is the heart of our faith and the living nerve of our worship.

> Behold, the Eternal King and Priest
> Brings forth for me the Bread and Wine.

VIII

DEATH AND THE AGE TO COME

THE CHRISTIAN DOCTRINE OF THE
LAST THINGS

THIS is the last of the lectures which I have been privileged to give here this term. As you know, they have been addressed to men and women of all faculties; people whose specialized interests are strikingly varied. Some of us are historians or economists; some read the classics or modern languages; some do highly technical work in laboratories.

But there is one intellectual interest common to us all. Indeed, the word 'intellectual' is not wide enough to describe it, since it is common to all human beings whether they think systematically about it or not. No living man avoids it, any more than he avoids food or sleep. Like the man in the great comedy who had been talking prose all his life without knowing it, we are all doing one thing willy-nilly, in virtue of facts which make man man, and differentiate him from stone or cabbage or the most intelligent chimpanzee that ever was. Trite though the remark is, we are all interpreting the Universe and trying to make sense of it. We are all looking at our world to discover what is the most significant thing about it. We look before and after. Men may not read books or enter laboratories, but in the very act of living the human life they seek wisdom, since wisdom means the capacity to understand things as a whole.

Indeed, man is the only part of creation known to us which is able to reflect about the ultimate meaning of creation.

Creation's 'ultimate' meaning; that is, its meaning as disclosed by its end, its final purpose and outcome. This is the real meaning of anything. Aristotle, in the *Physics* and the *Politics*, taught that the nature of a thing is determined not so much by its rudimentary stage as by its final stage, its τέλος or end. The word is used not only in the chronological, but in the metaphysical sense. The real meaning of the alphabet is given by the sentence. The true nature of this block of marble is the finished statue. A saw is made of steel: why not of putty or brown paper? Why not by the famous engineering firm of Heath Robinson? Because its end is to cut timber, or even iron. Its end alone explains its beginning. The completeness of a thing, says Aristotle, determines its nature.

What, then, is the ultimate meaning of man's life? What does the glittering tumult of human history, the glory and tragedy of the human centuries, all come to? The cynic has answered that life is a comedy to him who thinks, and a tragedy to him who feels. The religious man answers that it is a victory for him who believes. Believes what? What may we believe about the problem which has vexed thought and tried faith in every generation, namely, the problem of Death? It is no mere play upon words to say that man's life is only to be evaluated in terms of its end. Making sense of life means, ultimately and always, making sense of Death.

In the first place, Death is the one certain fact. Philip of Macedon had a slave to whom he gave a standing order. The man was to come in to the King every morning of his life, no matter what the King was doing, and to say to him in a loud voice: 'Philip, remember that thou must die.' The story is a parable because it speaks to Everyman, not only to sceptre and crown, but to tinker and tailor. Death is the only prediction which we can make about human history with absolute certainty. Prediction is one of the marks of a natural science, admittedly. If hydrochloric acid is poured on to zinc in the Cambridge laboratories a hundred years hence, we know that hydrogen will be given off and zinc chloride will remain. Indeed, other things being equal, we can predict by means of statistical averages a number of numerical facts about society, its births, marriages and deaths, for example, in some given period. But is there any certainty that other things will remain equal? They are very unequal at the present moment of world history. The great imponderables are as much a factor of world history as the facts which may be expressed in terms of statistical averages. Wars do not necessarily go according to formula. The laws of mathematical probability have no obvious relation to my neighbour's experience when a time-bomb drops in his backyard rather than in mine. The fact is that we cannot predict what will happen to us or to our world, even one day ahead. Much is highly probable, but nothing is certain, except ultimate death, soon or late. The literature of the race is one long testimony to the mystery and pathos of man's mortality. Like *Hamlet*, it is full of quotations, stock quotations, all but one of which I will spare you. Here is a man, a great Elizabethan, brought to the block. His last words were to the headsman who was hesitating: 'Why dost thou not strike? Strike, man!' But Sir Walter Raleigh's last word is really that last magnificent sentence of his unfinished *History of the World*, written there in the Tower: 'O eloquent, just and mighty Death! whom none could advise, thou hast persuaded; what none hath dared, thou hast done; and whom all the world hath flattered, thou only hast cast out of the world and despised. Thou hast drawne together all the farre stretched greatnesse, all the pride, crueltie and ambition of man, and covered it all over with these two narrow words: *Hic Jacet*!'

In the second place, Death is the supremely tragic fact. By 'tragic' I do not mean 'sad', a popular misuse of language. I mean that there is an irresolvable, inexplicable contradiction or tension in every human death. Man is not only conscious of the fact of death; that consciousness is his alone. The experience which equates him with animals and plants, at the same time sets him high above them. He thinks he was not made to die. Like Cleopatra, he has immortal longings in him. If he is meant to perish, as 'sheep or goats, that nourish a blind life within the brain', why is he tortured with dreams, and creative heroisms; with noble disinterestedness and, above all, with love, which makes bereavement his immemorial agony? If Death is the Everlasting No, striking him down to dust inexorably at the last, why is there an Everlasting Yea in his heart? What power has written this irrational and mocking gloss into his very constitution? If death means that all is over and there is nothing more, it is life which is pervaded with tragic irrationality. Every column in the great human tot-book adds up to precisely the same result, Zero. '...Alles was entsteht ist wert dass es zu Grunde geht.' Mephistopheles there tells Faust that the value of everything is ultimately nothing. He exploits the tragic enigma, that human values are not only gloriously affirmed by our empirical life in time; they are also basely denied. Their enemy is sin, but their last victorious enemy is Death.

Human death may not be explained and dismissed as a purely natural phenomenon, a biological fact which touches man as closely as it touches the bird or the beaver. Death cannot be a purely natural fact for one who is not a purely natural being, but a person made in God's image. May I presume to quote something I wrote in a recent volume, entitled *Facing the Facts*: 'There is a world of difference between "dying" (a purely zoological fact, admittedly), and "having to die" (which is uniquely and poignantly human).... Physical death as such is not a problem; granted. But having to die is: it is the supreme illustration of the incomprehensibility of our world'? Death is 'the burden and the mystery of all this unintelligible world', just because Wordsworth and Everyman know they have to die.

In the third place, Death is a universal fact, claiming the human race itself. It is arguable that what we call 'Nature', which was here before man, will be here when man has gone, and the insubstantial pageant of his history is no more. Even the Pyramids, his own monument, may conceivably outlast him, as Toynbee suggests. The Squinancy Wort was there on the high downs before man; you may know the lines which Edward Carpenter puts into the mouth of the little flower:

> What have I done? Man came,
> Evolutional upstart one!
> With the gift of giving a name
> To everything under the sun.
> What have I done? Man came,
> (They say nothing sticks like dirt)
> Looked at me with eyes of blame
> And called me Squinancy Wort...

Yet there is hope; I have seen
Many changes since I began.
The web-footed beasts have been
(Dear beasts!) and gone, being part of some wider plan.
Perhaps in His infinite mercy, God will remove this Man!

Well, perhaps man, who is not only a fool but a sinner, may
remove himself. In any case, Christian doctrine will have
nothing to do with an earthly eternity for the human race, as
though the City of God were the goal of secular evolution here
on this planet, where men will live happily ever afterwards.
And this is the main answer which Christian doctrine makes to
Positivists such as Auguste Comte and George Eliot, and to all
whose evaluation of life's meaning is exclusively sociological.
The Positivists argued that though death is a grim fact allowing
no immortality to the individual, immortality is racial. We live
on in those who come after us; when a man dies he bequeathes
his record to the common stock of humanity; thus alone does he
find what Comte calls 'subjective immortality'. There is no
God: that 'stage', says Comte, is now over. Humanity is the
only God, the only Object of religion. Humanity is the one
Great Being. We mortals become 'his' objective servants in life
and then 'his' subjective organs after death. We 'transmit,
improved, to those who shall come after, the increasing heritage
we received from those who went before'. One might call it
'Immortality by metaphysical fiction': 'Immortality which is
always vicarious and never real.'

It is obvious that there is truth here. I mean that this worth-
less metaphysic is built on fact, the social solidarity of the
successive generations. In George Eliot's poem, where the
metaphysic is merely implicit, this truth receives a moving

presentation; like Stoicism, it bears itself nobly. Life to come, she says, is to 'be the sweet presence of a good diffused'; 'to be to other souls the cup of strength in some great agony...'. The poem is really a prayer, not to God of course, but to George Eliot:

> O may I join the choir invisible
> Of those immortal dead who live again
> In minds made better by their presence: live
> In pulses stirred to generosity,
> In deeds of daring rectitude: in scorn
> For miserable aims that end with self...
>
> So shall I join the choir invisible
> Whose music is the gladness of the world.

The admission which this splendidly audacious rhetoric barely conceals, is that these immortal dead are alive only by a poetic fiction. Objectively considered they have perished for ever. The choir is invisible because it is non-existent, not because it is the multitude of the heavenly host, unseen but eternal, singing a new song about the throne of God and of the Lamb.

To anticipate the next main section of this lecture for a moment, the Christian doctrine of the Last Things is always affirming one great truth, through all its varied imagery, namely, that the only true evaluation of this world is one which recognizes the impermanence of this world. Here we have no abiding city; we seek one that is to come, beyond history and beyond death. We are always strangers and sojourners; our citizenship is in Heaven.

Theology is here nearer to facts than the Utopian Ideologies of the modern age. History knows little of the dogma of inevitable progress from primitive barbarism to the perfect

human society. It traces the rise and fall of successive civilizations. It has its own concrete way of illustrating what Christian
doctrine knows as Original Sin. Further, philosophy rightly
reminds evolutionary optimists, with their explicitly secularist,
this-worldly presuppositions, that such doctrinaire optimism is
only another name for a most ghastly pessimism. The worst
totalitarianism of all would be one which, beginning in 'the
dark backward and abysm of time' and going on and on into a
far distant future, cheerfully and ruthlessly sacrifices the toiling,
sorrowing, dying generations of men to eternal death, that the
last and luckiest generations may reach the Earthly Paradise—
the end to which all this is the means—before they too go down
in the darkness of death and annihilation. William Morris'
News from Nowhere come true, for three-score years and ten, or
perchance four- or even five-score years! Would Death be less
or more tragic in such a world of perfect justice and happiness?
Against such a background of felicity in a planet of garden
cities, William Watson's cry would surely be more, not less,
agonizing:

> But ah! to know not while with friends I sit,
> And while the purple joy is passed about,
> Whether 'tis ampler day divinelier lit
> Or homeless night without.

> And whether, stepping forth, my soul shall see
> New prospects, or fall sheer—a blinded thing:
> There is, O Grave, thy hourly victory,
> And there, O Death, thy sting.

In the fourth place, Death is the one inescapable fact which
compels men to choose between despair and faith.

Here the notorious problem of evil comes to a head; it reaches its climax, its breaking point. Here and here only we see the meaning of its stark inescapability. The problem is mainly two-fold. There is first, metaphysical evil; that is, man's sense of finitude and transitoriness, to which I have been drawing your attention all along. Well, it all comes to its maximum intensity here. It is seen for what it is against the vast, empty, senseless nothingness of Death. Death is, as a modern philosopher has put it, 'the supreme external manifestation of temporality'. One might say that it is the sacrament of time, time's most effectual sign. Secondly, there is moral evil; that is, man's sense of failure, sin and guilt. For all this, too, death is the supreme crisis. Crisis is a Greek word meaning Judgment. The Apostle wrote that the sting of death is sin. Why? Well the life-long drama of the soul here comes to a climax which is inevitable, inescapable, unrehearsable, unanalysable, final. Here, everything constituting life's record is seen to be unalterable, indelible, irremediable. Death has been called the sacrament of sin because it is the effective sign of opportunities gone for ever. Death is tremendous because life is, and because in it life says its last word. Little wonder that James Denney, in protesting against the modern tendency to make light of human death, should have added that 'it is the greatest thought of which we are capable, except the thought of God'. The fact which is here inescapable is a dilemma. Either we despair, or we believe. There is no middle course, no razor-edge of non-committal on which to balance precariously. Only he who believes in God wins the victory over despair. Only the infinite mercy of the Eternal Love, incarnate, suffering, dying, rising from the dead, is big enough for the tragedy of human existence. The dilemma is inescapable.

Either despair which is Hell, or faith in him who giveth us the victory.

Christian eschatology is the outcome of such a faith. The doctrine of the end of history and of the life of the age to come is the form taken by teleology in the Hebraic-Christian tradition. Because it seeks to make sense of things, every philosophy includes a teleology of some sort; that is, a doctrine of ultimate meanings or ends. It is true that the word 'teleology' is not derived from the Greek τέλος (meaning 'end'), but from τέλειος (meaning 'perfect' or 'complete'). But the difference is negligible. The real meaning of anything, as we have already noticed, is determined by what it is when completed or perfected; that is, when it has reached the end which was implicit in its very beginning.

What is the meaning of human history, the life of the whole human race? To the Hebrews, with their realism and their interest in history, teleology took the special form of eschatology, a doctrine of the End, when the evil of the world will be judged and righted by God himself. The prophets always expected this 'Day of the Lord' which should consummate and fully reveal the divine purpose being worked out in history. By fixing their vision on the End, the Prophets were able to hold on to their faith that the whole of history is divinely ordered. They interpreted the darkest hour of the battle in the light of the coming victory, God's victory. The Present Age, with all its woe and sin, will give place to the Age to Come, a supernatural, supra-historical order of existence which will be the Lord's doing. In one sense, this Day of the Lord, ushering in the new Age, is the last of the long series of historical events, the final link in the chain, the last note which makes a unity of the scale. But, in another sense, to quote Professor Dodd, 'it is not an event in history at all; for it is described in terms which remove it from the conditions of time and space....It is such that no other event either could follow or need follow upon it, because in it the whole purpose of God is revealed and ful-filled.'[1] History thus reaches its goal, its absolute end, with the fulfilment of the divine purpose in creation.

But, how can there be an end to historic time? The idea is surely inconceivable; is it not therefore meaningless? We met precisely the same intellectual difficulty about the idea of a beginning of time, in creation. To conceive of such a beginning is just as impossible as to conceive of no beginning; similarly, to conceive of an end, when the eternal clock stops, so to speak, is as impossible as to conceive of no end, with the clock ticking away for ever and ever. As Dr Edwyn Bevan reminded us in his Gifford Lectures, the attempt to define or understand time is doomed to failure because time is wholly unique, something so wholly unlike anything else we know that when we try to explain it we find ourselves bringing terms of temporal signifi-cance into our explanation. Our definitions are necessarily circular, presupposing a knowledge of the very thing to be defined. This is what Augustine meant when he said: 'If nobody asks me what time is, I know: if I want to explain it to anyone who asks me, I am at a loss.'

The idea, then, of an absolute end to history, the End of the World, or the Last Judgment, is a *Grenzbegriff*, a symbol standing for the limit of all our conceiving; like the words *Ne plus ultra* on the maps of the old geographers. Eschatology is a symbolic way of expressing the reality of God's purpose within history. Like the Hebrew, and unlike the Greek, the Christian

[1] *The Apostolic Preaching*, p. 198.

knows that time matters; that history is God's roaring loom. That is why eschatology is the Christian teleology. Just as no living man knows or can know what death is, in all its mysterious nature and extent, so no man knows or can conceive what the end of history is. Everyman, whether he be an Old Testament prophet like Jeremiah or a New Testament apostle like St Paul; whether he be an H. G. Wells with his Time-Machine or an Eddington with his mathematical symbolism, Everyman is compelled to think here in terms of images. The vital point is that the symbolic imagery of the Bible always describes the End in terms of the supernatural, the eternal, the 'wholly-other'. The ultimate nature and meaning of history is only disclosed in its End, where God 'takes it up' as it were, into eternity, and it is seen to be part of eternity. To quote Professor Dodd again, the End 'is such that nothing more could happen in history because the eternal meaning which gives reality to history is now exhausted. To conceive any further event on the plane of history would be like drawing a cheque on a closed account.'[1] That is, the present Age ends with an Event which is itself the beginning of something new, the Age to Come, the Kingdom of God in all its perfection and glory.

The emphasis of Christian eschatology is thus two-fold; it makes an amazing statement which can be expressed only in the form of a dialectical tension or paradox.

On the one hand it proclaims that the End has already been realized. The Word became flesh, and dwelt among us, and we beheld his glory. The New Testament rings with this proclamation that the final outcome of history has already happened. The Age to Come is here, with power and great glory. That which was spoken by the prophet is come to pass. If any man is

[1] *The Apostolic Preaching*, p. 206.

in Christ there the new Creation, the Age to Come, is. He has tasted of its powers. Christ has rescued us out of the dominion of darkness and transferred us into the Kingdom of the Son of his love. The Kingdom of God has come upon us. Now is the crisis of this world: now is the Prince of this world cast out. This is the Judgment, that the Light has come into the world, and men love darkness rather than the light. The one far-off divine event to which the whole creation moves has burst into human history, in the coming, the miraculous ministry, the death and the resurrection of Jesus Christ. Christ is risen from the dead, the firstfruits of the Age to Come. We are raised with him in newness of life. He who believes on him has eternal life. This coming of the Incarnate Word is the decisive End; old things are passed away, all things henceforward are new; that is, different in quality. The whole human race stands in a new relation to the temporal, historic order; the old relation is broken and there can never be any going back to it. To attempt to do so is to be judged; it is to prefer the provisional to the absolute which has displaced it. Jesus Christ is the unique and final impact of the Kingdom of God on human experience; to go back behind it is as impossible as to go beyond it.

But, on the other hand (and this is what makes the dialectical tension), human history does not cease to be history, under the forms of time and sense, even though our life is now eternal life, and we sit in heavenly places with Christ. We still live in the body; we still sin; we still have to die. Ideally or potentially considered, our life is lived with Christ in God. But empirically considered, our life is still 'in the flesh'. The Kingdom of God has come; the Eternal Now has been given to our experience; the New Testament is a monument to this fact. Nevertheless, the New Testament also looks to a future consummation, a final judgment, an End which is 'not yet', an eternal order of blessedness in God of which our Christian life in time is the foretaste and the firstfruits. Thus, the Age to Come is a present experience; and yet it is a future consummation; that is the paradox of New Testament eschatology. How is it to be understood or resolved? Redemption, as we have seen, must mean redemption from Death, if it is to be a reality which matters. But this does not imply simply more life after death. That would have been nothing new to most Jews of the time when the Gospel was first preached. The life and immortality brought to light by the Gospel are not quantity but quality. All turns on quality, that eternal life of which the New Testament speaks and which is begun now, that it may reach its fruition hereafter under new conditions. We still have to die: but Death changes its meaning when a man knows that he has already tasted of the life beyond its portals (ζωὴ αἰώνιος).

There is the paradox. The New Testament speaks, therefore, not only of Christ's coming in Bethlehem, nineteen centuries ago, but also of his second coming. Christian doctrine teaches a *geminus adventus*, a two-fold advent, reminding men that the Christian life is lived in terms of this tension, between what has happened and what will happen; between this world where we have surely seen the light of the knowledge of God's glory on the face of Christ and the world to come where the whole meaning of Christian history as the accomplishment of God's purpose will be revealed in the Last Judgment. This tension, which the *geminus adventus* illustrates, can only be set forth in terms of a dialectic which holds together present experience and future hope. Indeed, the Christian hope cannot be precisely described; it can only be 'pictured' in symbolical language, suggested by the varied imagery of different New Testament writers. Such language wrestles with ineffable things lying beyond the utmost range of all human experience, things which 'eye hath not seen nor ear heard'. The drama of the Last Judgment takes place in the eternal world, to which Death is the inevitable and only gateway.

Christian eschatology means that the true evaluation of this world must rest against the background of its impermanence. 'Otherworldliness' is the differentia of Christian life in this world. Neville Figgis used to say that the core of the Gospel, the very essence of the Christian life, is 'otherworldliness'. He was in line, of course, with the New Testament and with Christian doctrine. Here we have no abiding city. We seek a better country, that is, a heavenly. Moreover, Figgis was in line with the New Testament and with Christian doctrine in insisting that here is the true motive for Christian social action. 'The heavenly life alone', he wrote, 'lends reality to all schemes of earthly amelioration; the life beyond which alone gives value to this; the eternal, the immortal, the invisible, which alone makes it worth while to lift mankind from the mire of selfishness and corruption. . . . Only as we live within the circle of the Ascended Glory shall we really be able for work here.'[1] Christian doctrine is unmistakably explicit about 'the life of the Age to Come', for which the Church of God on earth is preparation, forehint and foretaste. The Holy Spirit by which the Church lives is, here and now, the earnest of a heavenly inheritance. And I venture to add that we have too long halted in this matter in 'implicits' and should come out far more than we do into 'explicits'. For by now the development of the human situation is curing us, and seems like to

[1] From an article by F. J. E. Raby in *Theology*, May 1940.

cure us even more drastically, of trying to put the Catholic and Evangelical Churchmanship of the Christian ages into an exclusive context of social or world improvement, or other such alien ideology. It has to go back into the context which belongs to it and to which it belongs, namely the unworldly, if not the other-worldly, one. Bunyan's characteristic word, 'the milk and honey is beyond this wilderness', is what all great Christians have said, Christians whom no one may charge with being ineffectives while they were on this side of Jordan river. 'In Egypt, Rome and Carthage it was the custom to deliver to the candidates at their first communion, in addition to bread and wine, a cup of milk and honey, to give them a foretaste of the heavenly food of which the blessed partake in the Kingdom of God.'[1] The manna in the wilderness is never an end in itself. It points beyond itself; it is heavenly food; it is the foretaste as well as the promise, of the feast in the heavenly Kingdom.

Therefore I am neither afraid nor ashamed to remind you that Christian doctrine may never forget the sane but quite definite otherworldliness, which is one indisputable aspect of our religion in all its transcendent absoluteness. Our citizenship is in heaven. Its centre is in God. This is true of original Christianity; this is the unmistakable implication of our Churchmanship, and it has immense relevance to the predicament in which we now are.

The urgency of the issues raised by eschatology is obvious. Does the Christian faith matter? If so, how much does it matter? If it does not matter vitally and urgently, does it matter at all? Consider these moving words: 'But above all for

---

[1] *Cambridge Ancient History,* xii. 527.

thine inestimable love in the redemption of the world by our Lord Jesus Christ, for the means of grace, and for the hope of glory.' As a sinful man looking at death and beyond it, into the eternal world, I need salvation. Nothing else will meet my case. There is something genuinely at stake in every man's life, the climax whereof is death. Dying is inevitable, but arriving at the destination God offers to me is not inevitable. It is not impossible to go out of the way and fail to arrive. Christian doctrine has always urged that life eternal is something which may conceivably be missed. It is possible to neglect this great salvation and to lose it eternally, even though no man may say that anything is impossible with God or that his grace may ultimately be defeated.[1]

I know it is no longer fashionable to talk about Hell, one good reason for this being that to make religion into a prudential insurance policy is to degrade it. The Faith is not a fire-escape. But in rejecting the old mythology of eternity as grotesque and even immoral, many people make the mistake of rejecting the truth it illustrated (which is rather like rejecting a book as untrue because the pictures in it are bad). It is illogical to tell men that they must do the will of God and accept his gospel of grace, if you also tell them that the obligation has no eternal significance, and that nothing ultimately depends on it. The curious modern heresy that everything is bound to come right in the end is so frivolous that I will not insult you by refuting it. 'I remember', said Dr Johnson on one occasion, 'that my Maker has said that he will place the sheep on his right hand and the goats on his left.' That is a solemn truth

---

[1] The substance and phrasing of this and the succeeding paragraph are taken largely from one of my chapters in *The Way to God*, by permission of the S.C.M. Press.

which only the empty-headed and empty-hearted will neglect. It strikes at the very roots of life and destiny.

My lectures are at an end. I am acutely conscious of their many omissions and defects; but I am more conscious of the encouragement you have given me by honouring them so signally with your presence and attention.

BIBLIOGRAPHY

The general reader who is not a specialist in theology may find a guide for further reading in these lists of books:

GENERAL

BRUNNER, E. *Our Faith* (Harpers).
DENNEY, J. *Studies in Theology* (Hodder; out of print).
GARVIE, A.E. *The Christian Doctrine of the Godhead* (Hodder).
KIRK, K. (editor). *The Study of Theology* (Hodder), with special reference to the opening chapter contributed by N. P. Williams.
MATTHEWS, W.R. (editor). *The Christian Faith* (Eyre & Spottiswoode).
QUICK, O.C. *Doctrines of the Creed* (Nisbet).

I. BELIEF IN GOD

BAILLIE, J. *Our Knowledge of God* (Oxford).
FARMER, H.H. *The World and God* (Nisbet).
GORE, C. *The Philosophy of the Good Life* (Everyman).
MATTHEWS, W.R. *God in Christian Thought and Experience* (Nisbet).
ROBINSON, H.W. *The Religious Ideas of the Old Testament* (Duckworth).
TAYLOR, A.E. Essay in *Essays Catholic and Critical* (S.P.C.K.).

II. MAN AND SIN

BRUNNER, E. *Man in Revolt* (Lutterworth).
OXFORD CONFERENCE. *The Christian Understanding of Man* (Allen & Unwin).
HORTON, W.M. *Realistic Theology* (Hodder).
LEWIS, C.S. *The Problem of Pain* (Centenary).
NIEBUHR, R. *An Interpretation of Christian Ethics* (S.C.M.).
ROBINSON, H.W. *The Christian Doctrine of Man*, 2nd ed. (Clark).
TAYLOR, A.E. *The Faith of a Moralist*, vol. I, chap. v (Macmillan).
WHALE, J.S. *The Christian Answer to the Problem of Evil* (S.C.M.).
WILLIAMS, N.P. *The Ideas of the Fall and of Original Sin* (Longmans).

III. History and the Kingdom of God

BERDYAEV, N. *The Meaning of History* (Centenary).
BEVAN, E. *Christianity* (Thornton Butterworth).
DODD, C.H. *The Parables of the Kingdom* (Nisbet).
—— *The Apostolic Preaching* (Hodder).
OXFORD CONFERENCE. *The Kingdom of God and History* (Allen & Unwin).
WEBB, C.C.J. *The Historical Element in Religion* (Allen & Unwin).
WOOD, H.G. *Christianity and the Meaning of History* (Cambridge).

IV. The Work of Christ

AULÉN, G. *Christus Victor* (S.P.C.K.).
CAVE, S. *The Doctrine of the Work of Christ* (Hodder).
DENNEY, J. *The Death of Christ* (Hodder).
FRANKS, R.S. *The Atonement* (Oxford).
MACKINTOSH, H.R. *The Christian Experience of Forgiveness* (Nisbet).
TAYLOR, V. *Jesus and His Sacrifice* (Macmillan).

V. The Person of Christ

BARTLET, J.V. Three chapters in *The Lord of Life* (S.C.M.).
BRUNNER, E. *The Mediator* (Lutterworth).
CAVE, S. *The Doctrine of the Person of Christ* (Duckworth).
FORSYTH, P.T. *The Person and Place of Jesus Christ* (Independent).
GORE, C. *Belief in Christ* (Murray).
LOOFS, F. *What is the Truth about Jesus Christ?* (Clark).
RAWLINSON, A.E.J. *The New Testament Doctrine of the Christ* (Longmans).

VI. The Church

CALVIN. *Institutes*, Book IV, translated by H. Beveridge (Calvin Translation Society).
EHRENSTRÖM, N. *Christian Faith and the Modern State* (S.C.M.).
FLEW, R.N. *Jesus and His Church* (Epworth).
HORT, F.J.A. *The Christian Ecclesia* (Macmillan).
LUTHER. *Primary Works*, translated by Wace and Buchheim (Hodder).
OLDHAM, J.H. and HOOFT, V.'T. *The Church and its Function in Society* (Allen & Unwin).
OMAN, J. *The Church and the Divine Order* (Hodder).
STREETER, B.H. *The Primitive Church* (Macmillan).

VII. The Word and the Sacraments

BARCLAY, A. *The Protestant Doctrine of the Lord's Supper* (Glasgow).

DALE, R.W. *Manual of Congregational Principles* (Independent).

Encyclopaedia of Religion and Ethics. Articles on Eucharist, Sacraments and Worship.

HEADLAM, A.C. and DUNKERLEY, R. (editors). *The Ministr and the Sacraments* (S.C.M.).

MAXWELL, W.D. *An Outline of Christian Worship* (Oxford).

MICKLEM, N. (editor). *Christian Worship* (Oxford).

MOZLEY, J.K. *The Gospel Sacraments* (Hodder).

SCHENCK, L.B. *The Presbyterian Doctrine of Children in the Covenant* (Yale).

VIII. The Last Things

BAILLIE, J. *And the Life Everlasting* (Oxford).

CHARLES, R.H. *Eschatology: Hebrew, Jewish and Christian* (Black).

COMMISSION REPORT. *Doctrine in the Church of England* (S.P.C.K.).

DODD, C.H. *The Apostolic Preaching*, Appendix (Hodder).

MATTHEWS, W.R. *The Hope of Immortality* (S.C.M.).

VON HÜGEL, F. *Essays and Addresses*, No. 7 (Dent).

INDEX

191